2,001 Ways to Pamper Yourself

Lorraine Bodger

Lorraine Bodger's
other books include:

A Year of Cookies

Chocolate Cookies

Chicken Dinners

The Christmas Kitchen

Gift Wraps

Christmas Tree Ornaments

Woman's Day Doughcrafts

Crafts for All Seasons

Paper Dreams

2,001 Ways

to Pamper Yourself

Lorraine Bodger

**Andrews McMeel
Publishing**

Kansas City

2,001 Ways to Pamper Yourself copyright © 1999 by
Lorraine Bodger. All rights reserved. Printed in Hong Kong.
No part of this book may be used or reproduced in any
manner whatsoever without written permission except in
the case of reprints in the context of reviews. For
information, write Andrews McMeel Publishing, an
Andrews McMeel Universal company, 4520 Main Street,
Kansas City, Missouri 64111.

www.andrewsmcmeel.com

Library of Congress Cataloging-in-Publication Data

Bodger, Lorraine.
        2,001 ways to pamper yourself / Lorraine Bodger .
        p.   cm.
        ISBN 0-7407-0022-7 (pbk.)
        1. Conduct of life—Miscellanea. 2. Self-actualization
(Psychology)   I. Title.   II. Title: Two thousand and
one ways to pamper yourself.
BJ1595.B625 1999   99-331199
158.1—dc21   CIP

Book design by Lisa Martin

Introduction

Pampering, contrary to popular wisdom, is not *bad* for you—it's *wonderful* for you! It's one of the best things that can happen to you. Pampering doesn't mean spoiling. It means indulging, caretaking, making you feel good, delighting you, bringing you joy. Pampering makes you remember that you're a person worth pampering, a person who deserves to be well taken care of.

You *do* deserve to be pampered, and not just when you've gotten a raise or won the Nobel Prize. You have a right to be pampered any time you need it, any day of the week, summer, winter, spring, and fall—in big ways and in little ways, from the sublime to the maybe-it's-silly-but-it-makes-me-feel-good ridiculous.

Wouldn't it be wonderful if there were a person on call twenty-four hours a day for pampering duty? There is—and that person is you. After all, who knows better than you exactly what you need? Exactly what you feel like doing? Exactly what would make you happy at this very moment?

In this book you'll find hundreds and hundreds of marvelous ways to satisfy your desire to be pampered, to give yourself as much kindness and comfort, pleasure and fun as a person might hope to enjoy in one lifetime.

· 1 ·
Choose three fabulous chocolate truffles
and savor them slowly.

· 2 ·
Give yourself a day off during the week.
Stay in bed and do nothing.

· 3 ·
Take a scented bath by candlelight.

· 4 ·
Rake leaves on a crisp fall morning when
the sky is cobalt blue and there's a faint
smell of wood smoke in the air.

· 5 ·
Hire a professional to help you
organize your closet.

· 6 ·

Call a car service instead of taking
the bus or subway.

· 7 ·

Go to a romantic movie in the afternoon.

· 8 ·

Make love in the afternoon.

· 9 ·

Drive a Harley-Davidson as fast
as the law allows.

· 10 ·

Subscribe to a magazine you've
always wanted.

· 11 ·

Telephone your closest friend and
talk as long as you like.

❀ Do yourself a favor:
Throw away every item of your clothing
that doesn't look *great* on you.

· 13 ·

Go on a house tour and swoon over
the gorgeous interiors. Then go home
and be glad you don't have to take
care of all that stuff.

· 14 ·

Have bagels, cream cheese, and
lox on Sunday morning.

· 15 ·

Instead of milk, put
cream in your coffee.

· 16 ·

Take the time to build a roaring
fire in your fireplace.

· 17 ·

Make twice as much popcorn
as you can eat.

· 18 ·

Let your partner massage your feet.

· 19 ·

Curl up and reread your favorite novel.

· 20 ·

Read a novel you've always
meant to pick up.

· 21 ·

Read a biography of someone
you admire.

· 22 ·

Reread the book you loved most
when you were nine.

✳ *Give yourself a break:*
Stop looking backward with longing. Start
looking forward with anticipation.

· 24 ·

Take a child to a petting zoo—
so *you* can pet the animals.

· 25 ·

Visit a museum and treat yourself to a
wonderful lunch in the museum café.

· 26 ·

Put a "Do Not Disturb" sign
on your office door.

· 27 ·

Put a "Do Not Disturb" sign
on your bedroom door.

· 28 ·

Have your broken jewelry repaired.

· 29 ·

If you've got a secret yearning
for the footlights, try out for a part in
your local theater group's next play.

· 30 ·

Make a list of everything in
your home that needs fixing,
and hire someone to do it.

· 31 ·

Use your answering machine to
screen your calls when you don't
feel like talking to anyone.

· 32 ·

Get Call Waiting.

· 33 ·

Get rid of Call Waiting.

· 34 ·

Buy fresh flowers every
week for a month.

· 35 ·

Try lavender cologne. It's said to
have a calming effect, and it's as fragrant
as a late summer day.

· 36 ·

Get a full body massage.

· 37 ·

Leaf through your old high school
yearbook and remember how it felt to
be sixteen. Be glad you're grown up.

· 38 ·

Let a professional makeup artist
give you a new look.

* *Go to the annual
family reunion.*

* *Don't go to the annual
family reunion.*

· 41 ·

Dress up and go swing dancing.

· 42 ·

Drop in at a jazz club and stay
until the wee hours.

· 43 ·

Get up early and go canoeing
with your sweetheart.

· 44 ·

Have an old-fashioned picnic,
complete with picnic basket, red-checked
cloth, and deviled eggs.

· 45 ·

Go apple picking in autumn,
berry picking in summer.

· 46 ·

Eat a ripe, sun-warmed tomato while
standing in your garden.

· 47 ·

Have an accountant or tax lawyer fill
out your tax return this year.

· 48 ·

Head for a comedy club and laugh till
you fall out of your chair.

· 49 ·

Raid the refrigerator
at midnight.

· 50 ·

Learn a craft you've always wanted
to master: knitting, woodworking,
stenciling, needlepoint.

❀ *Do yourself a favor:*
Buy only water-soluble art
supplies for your kids.

· 52 ·

Throw a tantrum.

· 53 ·

Have dessert first.

· 54 ·

Take a laundry holiday—let it
pile up for two weeks!

· 55 ·

Go to a department store and try on
evening dresses just for the fun of it.

· 56 ·

When you're feeling fragile,
be good to yourself: Stick close to
familiar routines, eat your favorite foods,
see your best old friends.

· 57 ·

When you're feeling strong, be good to
yourself: Take on a new job, travel to a
new place, meet new people.

· 58 ·

Paint your bathroom the color
of the Mediterranean Sea.

· 59 ·

Take a yoga class.

· 60 ·

Take a stretch class.

· 61 ·

Buy yourself a snuggly
stuffed animal.

· 62 ·

Attend a wine tasting at a vineyard.

· 63 ·

Listen to audio books while
driving to work.

· 64 ·

Use as many self-stick notes as you want.

· 65 ·

Make yourself a present of the
cookbook you've been eyeing greedily
at the bookstore.

· 66 ·

Have your palm read.

· 67 ·

Don't be embarrassed if you've
shown your worst self. Your best self
will have its turn later.

· 68 ·

Be like water: If there's a crack, a path, or a
route for moving forward, water will find it.

· 69 ·

Watch the early Disney animated films:
*Fantasia, Cinderella, Snow White,
Bambi, Dumbo.*

· 70 ·

Ride a merry-go-round.

· 71 ·

Go skating in the moonlight.

· 72 ·

Pick wildflowers.

· 73 ·

Snag the Sunday paper before anyone else,
and do the crossword puzzle.

· 74 ·

Watch videos of the television
shows you loved when
you were a kid.

· 75 ·

Sing duets with Ella Fitzgerald,
Bonnie Raitt, or Dolly Parton.

· 76 ·

Learn salsa dancing.

· 77 ·

Scout a gourmet food shop for three
things you've never tasted before.
Take them home and try them.

· 78 ·

Visit a toy store and reminisce.

· 79 ·

Sit in a sculpture garden and meditate.

· 80 ·

Spend a weekend in a hotel in
your own city. Go sight-seeing.

· 81 ·

Order a champagne cocktail
in a dimly lit bar.

· 82 ·

Eat a whole jar of macadamia nuts.

· 83 ·

Subscribe to a concert series.

❀ *Give yourself a break:*
Don't try to do everything at once.

· 85 ·

Take your emotional temperature:
How are you feeling today? Do you want
quiet? Adventure? Comfort? Provide
yourself with whatever you need.

· 86 ·

Have a marathon movie session: Rent
three or four videotapes you've always
wanted to see, and watch them all.

· 87 ·

Make yourself a glass of
chocolate milk.

· 88 ·

Lounge on your porch on a
perfect summer night.

· 89 ·

Sit on a mountainside and
watch the sunset.

· 90 ·

Lie on a beach and watch the sunrise.

· 91 ·

Float in a pool.

· 92 ·

Listen to a recording of Mel Brooks
and Carl Reiner doing
The 2000-Year-Old Man.

· 93 ·

Have a manicure, and be sure it includes
a hand and arm massage.

· 94 ·

Have a pedicure, and be sure
it includes hot wax.

· 95 ·

Bake a batch of chocolate chip cookies
and keep them all for yourself.

· 96 ·

Once in a while, put on your pajamas or nightgown and bathrobe as soon as you arrive home from work. Relax.

· 97 ·

Have oatmeal for supper.

· 98 ·

Alphabetize your books.

❀ *Do yourself a favor:*

Organize *just one* bookshelf, drawer, or closet.

· 100 ·

Adopt a kitten.

· 101 ·

Adopt a puppy.

· 102 ·

Have someone bring you breakfast
in bed on your birthday.

· 103 ·

Try aromatherapy, with a diffuser
and a selection of essential oils.

· 104 ·

Buy yourself a wonderful new hairbrush.

· 105 ·

Treat yourself to a clock radio
with large numbers that you don't
have to squint to see.

· 106 ·

Pamper your cold feet with an
electric foot-of-the-bed warmer.

· 107 ·

Eat dinner by candlelight.

· 108 ·

Read a really great old mystery by
Agatha Christie, Dorothy Sayers,
or Josephine Tey.

· 109 ·

Read a really great new mystery by Sue
Grafton, Lawrence Block, or Steve Martini.

· 110 ·

Did you *love* that movie? Go see it again.

❀ *Give yourself a break:*

When everyone is driving you crazy, go into
your bedroom and shut the door. Stay there
until you feel better or they go away.

· 112 ·

Take a walk at dawn.

· 113 ·

Meet a friend for lunch.

· 114 ·

Bake an old-fashioned pound cake.

· 115 ·

Do not—repeat, *do not*—let rejection stop
you from heading in your chosen direction.
Learn what you can from it and move on.

✳ *Think before you act.*

✳ *Don't think before you act.*

· 118 ·

Watch a sad movie and cry
as much as you want.

· 119 ·

Clean your computer keyboard.

· 120 ·

Polish your silver jewelry
and admire the rich glow.

· 121 ·

On a cold winter night, turn on your heating
pad and put it between the sheets for at least
half an hour before you climb into bed.

· 122 ·

Curl up on the couch and read all
the interesting magazine articles
you've been saving.

· 123 ·

Make cuddling a part of every day.

· 124 ·

Take a scenic drive to the accompaniment
of your favorite CDs.

· 125 ·

Buy two pairs of shoes
instead of one.

· 126 ·

Eat peanut butter straight from the jar.

· 127 ·

Wash your new jeans ten times,
so they'll be nice and soft.

· 128 ·

Go fishing in a rowboat.

· 129 ·

Dig mussels or clams on a
secluded beach.

· 130 ·

Make real iced tea.

· 131 ·

See the Fourth of July fireworks.

❋ *Give yourself a break:*
Calm down. You don't have to be
the life of every party.

· 133 ·

Have a tall summer drink by the pool.

· 134 ·

Stock up on pretty wrapping paper,
ribbons, and gift tags.

· 135 ·

Buy so many stamps that you don't
have to go back to the post office
for at least three months.

· 136 ·

Read old love letters.

· 137 ·

Read a cutting-edge new novel.

· 138 ·

Wear lacy underthings.

· 139 ·

Throw out your flat old pillow
and buy a fluffy new one.

· 140 ·

Pamper your face with a soothing mask.

· 141 ·

Slather your whole body with moisturizer.

· 142 ·

Tuck a sachet into your sweater drawer.

· 143 ·

Have a chocolate milkshake.

· 144 ·

Host a pajama party.

· 145 ·

Play your favorite show tunes and sing
along at the top of your voice.

· 146 ·

Go to the ballet.

· 147 ·

Take tap-dancing lessons.

· 148 ·

Try a new eyeshadow.

· 149 ·

Buy the gadget you've always wanted.

· 150 ·

Get a new wallet with enough pockets
and slots for all the cards and other
things you absolutely need.

· 151 ·

Eat a jar of baby food.

· 152 ·

Paint your toenails.

· 153 ·

Wear comfortable shoes.

· 154 ·

Wrap yourself in a supersoft
cashmere scarf.

❀ *Do yourself a favor:*
Choose friends who support
and encourage you.

· 156 ·

Hire someone to wash your windows.

· 157 ·

Have dinner at a restaurant
with a spectacular view.

· 158 ·

Sleep out in the backyard on a
starry summer night.

* *Read the daily paper*
for a week.

* *Don't read the daily paper*
for a week.

· 161 ·

Enter a Ping-Pong tournament.

· 162 ·

Spend a quiet day alone, without talking.

· 163 ·

Make rice pudding.

· 164 ·

Have a kir royale—champagne
with a splash of cassis.

· 165 ·

Go window shopping.

· 166 ·
Test the mattresses in your
local department store.

· 167 ·
Invest in a great briefcase.

· 168 ·
Treat yourself to enough stationery
supplies to keep you from worrying about
running out: paper clips, self-stick
notes, pens, paper, envelopes.

· 169 ·
Read poetry.

· 170 ·
Write poetry.

· 171 ·
Brew a pot of real (loose) tea. Try Ceylon,
Assam, Darjeeling, English Breakfast,
Earl Grey, or green tea.

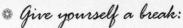

✴ Give yourself a break:
Slow down. Make no plans for the
upcoming weekend.

· 173 ·

Swim out as far as you can, and
look back at the shore. See how
small your problems are.

· 174 ·

Get a two-scoop ice cream cone
and take it for a stroll.

· 175 ·

Make angels in freshly fallen snow.

· 176 ·

Visit your oldest friend and reminisce.

· 177 ·

Take a vacation and don't give your
phone number to: the office, your
mother, your grown children.

· 178 ·

Attend an organ recital and get
carried away by the music.

· 179 ·

Take a white water rafting trip
and shoot the rapids.

· 180 ·

Drift down a lazy stream in an inner tube.

· 181 ·

Spend an afternoon antiquing.

· 182 ·

Go bowling with your girlfriends.

· 183 ·

Make yourself a big plate of spaghetti,
with olive oil and freshly grated
Parmesan cheese.

· 184 ·
Try on real Japanese kimonos.

· 185 ·
Send away for a fruit-of-the-month
or flower-of-the-month.

· 186 ·
Read Virginia Woolf's *A Room of One's
Own*, and then create a room for yourself.

· 187 ·
Hang out at a martini bar.

· 188 ·
Pin a rose to your tailored jacket.

· 189 ·
Engage a personal shopper for an afternoon.

· 190 ·
Sign up for a Spanish class.

❋ *Do yourself a favor:*
Enjoy where you are *right now.*

· 192 ·
Cool off like a kid: Dash into the lawn
sprinkler on a hot summer day.

· 193 ·
Order a pizza with your three
favorite toppings.

· 194 ·
Take a historical walking tour of your city.

· 195 ·
Have a friend or an expert connect your
VCR, and then program it—and teach
you how to program it too.

· 196 ·
Go sledding with your lover.

· 197 ·

Keep a bowl of candy on your desk.

· 198 ·

Stay at a rustic bed-and-breakfast
for a weekend.

· 199 ·

Wear a fuzzy,
warm bed jacket for reading in bed.

· 200 ·

Start a wish list or a wish folder. Anything
goes—wishes for world peace along with
wishes for diamond earrings.

· 201 ·

Do something that makes you feel like
a contributing member of society:
Teach someone to read or write, work
to clean up your local river or lake,
work on an election campaign.

· 202 ·

In February, fill a vase with tulips, to remind you that spring *will* come.

· 203 ·

Walk your bike to the top of the hill and coast down.

· 204 ·

Watch the seals cavort in the seal pond at the zoo.

· 205 ·

Play hopscotch with your kids.

· 206 ·

Buy yourself a great set of colored pencils.

· 207 ·

Treat yourself to a new toaster.

· 208 ·

Get into the glitz in Las Vegas
or Atlantic City.

· 209 ·

Swoon over a video romance: *Moonstruck,
Green Card, Casablanca, The English
Patient, West Side Story, Pride and
Prejudice, The Philadelphia Story,
An Officer and a Gentleman, The Piano.*

· 210 ·

Dress in lush fabrics: silk,
velvet, taffeta, lace.

· 211 ·

Fast and feast: Eat very little for a whole
day, then treat yourself to a terrific
dinner at your favorite bistro.

· 212 ·

Wear a flannel nightgown or pajamas to bed.

· 213 ·

Bake bread.

· 214 ·

Do for yourself a few of the things you'd
ordinarily do only for guests: Arrange fresh
flowers in a little vase on your night table.
Pick out half a dozen terrific books and
magazines for before-bed reading. Put
special soap in the bathroom.

· 215 ·

Plan to get up early on the weekend—
and then don't.

· 216 ·

Organize your CD collection in handsome
racks made of wood, Plexiglas,
or whatever suits your style.

· 217 ·

Have all your scissors sharpened.

· 218 ·

Go to the theater.

· 219 ·

Make hot chocolate—the real thing.

· 220 ·

Make a fresh pot of coffee
whenever you want it.

· 221 ·

Buy a new set of sheets and pillowcases
in a color or pattern unlike any
you've ever owned before.

· 222 ·

Change your hairstyle.

· 223 ·

Get a good reading
lamp to go on your
night table or beside your easy chair.

· 224 ·

Take a whale-watching trip off the
coast of California.

· 225 ·

Have a deep-cleaning facial.

· 226 ·

Have a mint julep.

· 227 ·

Go to Chinatown and order
a bowl of hot noodles.

· 228 ·

Pick out a new lipstick.

· 229 ·

Spend a day at a spa and try it all: loofah,
mud bath, head rub, the works.

· 230 ·

Make yourself a present of half a
dozen padded satin hangers.

· 231 ·

Stop in at a department store and spray
yourself with sensational cologne.

❀ *Do yourself a favor:*
If you see something you need, buy it.
Don't wait for another, better time.
There's no time like the present.

· 233 ·

Go to a sushi restaurant and—for once—
have all you can eat of the fish you love best.

· 234 ·

Wait until your significant other is out of
town for a few days, then gobble up all the
garlicky salami sandwiches you want.

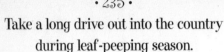

· 235 ·

Take a long drive out into the country
during leaf-peeping season.

✳ *Have a heart-to-heart talk*
with your mother.

✳ *Don't have a heart-to-heart*
talk with your mother.

· 238 ·

Treat yourself to an afternoon of
browsing through as many yard sales
as you can find.

· 239 ·

Lounge around the house in cozy
sweatpants and sweatshirt.

· 240 ·

Buy yourself a pound of pistachio nuts.

· 241 ·

Buy yourself a great fountain pen.

· 242 ·

Stroll through an art supply store
and feast your eyes on the colors.

· 243 ·

Eat with your fingers.

· 244 ·

Don't hedge your bets. Don't censor
your opinions. Don't hold back.

❀ *Do yourself a favor:*
Declare a twenty-four-hour
ban on complaining.

· 246 ·

Have dinner with your
favorite aunt.

· 247 ·

Carry an insulated container of homemade
soup or chili to work on a cold day.

· 248 ·

This year (finally) get yourself a pair of
superwarm winter boots.

· 249 ·

Crunch through the silent woods after a
fresh fall of snow.

· 250 ·

Set the table with a cloth, matching
napkins, and your best china—on
an ordinary weeknight.

· 251 ·

Rent an apartment or house in a foreign
country for a month, to get the
real flavor of living there.

· 252 ·

Wake up your taste buds with salsa
picante, pickled jalapeños, hot barbecue,
Szechuan food, a dab of wasabi, or
hot pepper flakes on your pizza.

· 253 ·

Wear black slacks to look thinner.

· 254 ·

Take a cool shower on a hot afternoon.

· 255 ·

Install good-looking ceiling fans.

· 256 ·

Spend a weekend afternoon viewing
houses for sale, even if you can't
afford to buy one right now.

· 257 ·

Get yourself a pair of leather sneakers.

· 258 ·

Join a specialty book club: mystery,
cooking, crafts, romance.

❀ *Do yourself a favor:*
Act confident even when you don't
feel confident. It helps.

· 260 ·

Outfit yourself glamorously
for your aerobics class.

· 261 ·

Twirl a baton in the Fourth of July parade.

· 262 ·

Put on your whites and play
croquet all afternoon.

· 263 ·

Buy that handsome tweed jacket
you've been eyeing.

· 264 ·

Walk out of a bad movie.

· 265 ·

Keep a bottle of champagne in the fridge
for unexpected special occasions.

· 266 ·

Keep a pitcher of iced coffee in the fridge
for summer pick-me-ups.

* *Have your ears pierced.*

* *Don't have your ears pierced.*

· 269 ·

Treat yourself to a loofah for the bath,
and a few natural sea sponges for
applying your makeup.

· 270 ·

Learn how to change the fuses or
throw the circuit breaker, so you'll
never be in the dark.

· 271 ·

Zip off on a short trip by moped.

· 272 ·

Order the biggest lobster.

· 273 ·

Ask for extra pickles.

· 274 ·

Fill out a Customer Satisfaction
card and tell the truth.

· 275 ·

Call a radio talk show and give the
host a piece of your mind.

· 276 ·

Ask your partner to read aloud to you.

· 277 ·

Give the cold shoulder to relatives
who are mean to you.

· 278 ·

Get a new flannel shirt and wash it a dozen
times to make it as soft as the old one.

· 279 ·

Treat yourself to a couple of
giant-size bath towels.

· 280 ·

Put a swimming pool in your backyard.

· 281 ·

Get ice cube trays that let the ice cubes
pop out without a struggle.

· 282 ·

Buy yourself a big box of assorted butter
cookies and eat one of each kind.

· 283 ·

Switch to low-fat milk.

· 284 ·

Go to a costume party in the
outfit you always wanted to wear
when you were a kid.

 Give yourself a break:
Do the best you can with any
problem, and if that doesn't
get results, move on.

· 286 ·

Break out of your routine
and make something new and
different for dinner.

· 287 ·

Break out of your routine and
make a date with someone
you haven't seen in ages.

· 288 ·

Break out of your routine and go
someplace you've never been before.

· 289 ·

Break out of your routine and
do something you never imagined
you could do.

· 290 ·

Read a book of short stories. Try John
Cheever, Gina Berriault, Andre Dubus,
Junichiro Tanizaki, Paule Marshall,
William Trevor, Elizabeth Jolley,
Raymond Carver, Grace Paley.

· 291 ·

Buy a good seat for a baseball game
in a park with real grass.

· 292 ·

Open a jar of mixed nuts. Eat all the
fancy ones and leave the peanuts.

· 293 ·

Have cocktails on the terrace.

· 294 ·

Grow tomatoes on your balcony.

· 295 ·

Hang overflowing pots of fuchsia
from the porch rafters.

· 296 ·

Climb a hill and get a wide view of the
world. Remember it *is* a wide world.

· 297 ·

Make the pilgrimage you've always dreamed
of—to Graceland, to Hollywood, to the
Vietnam Veterans Memorial in Washington,
D.C., to the home of the Brontë sisters.
Go where your heart leads.

· 298 ·

Use unexpected gifts of time (such as
canceled appointments) for treating yourself
to some impromptu pampering.

· 299 ·

Pamper yourself by pampering
the earth: Recycle.

· 300 ·

Close the door of your office and
do a few breathing exercises
and relaxing stretches.

· 301 ·
Put a spray of flowers in a
bud vase on your desk.

· 302 ·
Keep a list of the birthdays of
friends and family, so you don't
forget them and feel guilty.

· 303 ·

Buy yourself a
frosted cupcake.

· 304 ·
Reorganize your kitchen according
to how you *really* use it.

· 305 ·
Invest in a dishwasher that
actually does the job.

❋ *Give yourself a break:*
Let the dusting go for a week.

· 307 ·

Toss out your mix-and-don't-match
college flatware and buy a complete
set that you adore.

· 308 ·

Stop eating any food you don't like.

· 309 ·

Get up early and be the first on the beach.

· 310 ·

Stay late and be the last on the beach.

· 311 ·

Take the time to learn new software that
will enhance your life: personal accounting,
business or time management, writing
skills, or even graphic design.

· 312 ·

Back up your hard drive often.

· 313 ·

Take a snooze in a patch of sun
on the living room rug.

· 314 ·

Play the lottery game: What would
you do if you won the lottery?
Indulge your fantasies.

· 315 ·

Spend a week in London and go
to the theater every night.

· 316 ·

Make trifle in a handsome glass trifle bowl.

· 317 ·

Have a paperback book-buying
spree at a used book store.

· 318 ·

Get out of bed an hour before everyone
else, to enjoy sixty conscious minutes
of peace and quiet.

· 319 ·

Go on a week-long yoga retreat.

· 320 ·

Gather together all those cookbooks
you never use, and donate them to
a charity-run thrift shop.

· 321 ·

Pack up that huge pile of old
newspapers and recycle it.

· 322 ·

Clean out the cabinet under the
kitchen sink, so you don't have to say
"yuck" every time you open it.

· 323 ·

Make yourself a present of a
new down comforter.

❄ *Give yourself a break:*
This year let somebody else organize the
big birthday party, the family reunion, the
potluck supper, the Christmas pageant.

· 325 ·

Eat bread and butter sprinkled
with brown sugar.

· 326 ·

Have a parfait.

· 327 ·

Make a tape of your twenty
favorite songs.

· 328 ·

Play with electric trains.

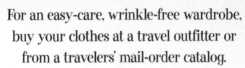

· 329 ·

For an easy-care, wrinkle-free wardrobe,
buy your clothes at a travel outfitter or
from a travelers' mail-order catalog.

· 330 ·

Pamper yourself with a pair of supersoft
sea-island cotton pajamas.

· 331 ·

Buy yourself a fabulous pair
of satin mules trimmed with
marabou feathers.

· 332 ·

Build a window seat, with padding and
cushions. Sit there and daydream.

· 333 ·

Throw caution to the winds: Ask that guy
you've had your eye on for a date.

· 334 ·

Sing duets with a friend who can
stay on key *and* do harmony.

· 335 ·

Make a vegetable garden and
don't plant zucchini.

· 336 ·

Book a ride in a glider plane.

· 337 ·

Enter your pet in a pet show.

· 338 ·

Go out for dinner without the kids.

· 339 ·

Watch the Oscars with a gang of
friends. Eat popcorn and candy,
drink soda, make bets on the winners,
cheer for your favorites.

· 340 ·

Feel free to be crabby.

❀ *Do yourself a favor:*
Stop apologizing for things that aren't
your fault or your responsibility.

· 342 ·

Move to another city to get away
from your past life.

· 343 ·

Hide from your responsibilities
for an afternoon.

· 344 ·

Take tango lessons.

· 345 ·

Go barefoot.

· 346 ·

Buy pretty stamps instead of plain ones.

· 347 ·

Keep a supply of interesting
postcards for writing short thank-yous,
notes, reminders.

· 348 ·

Live well. It's the best revenge.

· 349 ·

Throw out every pair of shoes
that makes your feet hurt.

· 350 ·

Have your hair streaked by a professional.

· 351 ·

Consider having cosmetic surgery.

· 352 ·

Send your family off on a
weekend trip while you stay home
and catch your breath.

· 353 ·

Have a package of Scottish
salmon all for yourself.

· 354 ·

Go to a millinery
supply store and put together
the hat of your dreams—a beautiful
basic form trimmed with feathers,
flowers, ribbons.

· 355 ·

Take a walk down Memory Lane:
Revisit your childhood home, your old
high school or college, the church where
you were married, the town where
your family used to summer.

· 356 ·

Ask a friend to listen to your troubles
without offering advice.

· 357 ·

Enroll in a class in financial
planning, to make yourself feel
confident and secure.

· 358 ·

Make your favorite foods for
dinner tonight.

· 359 ·

Lie in bed and listen to the
rain on the roof.

· 360 ·

Frame your favorite family photos
and hang them on a wall where you can
see and enjoy them every day.

· 361 ·

Take a carriage ride with your lover
and a bottle of good brandy.

· 362 ·

Treat yourself to a telephone (and a
calculator too) with large buttons, so you
don't have to strain to see the numbers.

· 363 ·

Hang a good mirror inside the door
of your coat closet for last-minute
checks before facing the world.

· 364 ·

Buy a dozen doughnut holes and don't share.

· 365 ·

Have someone snap a photo of you when
you have a great haircut. Show it to your
stylist next time you go in for a trim.

· 366 ·

Stash an extra set of
house and car keys at a friend's
place, so you'll never be locked out for long.

· 367 ·

Get reliable financial advice.

❀ *Give yourself a break:*
Prepare well ahead for that big
meeting or presentation, so you won't
be a nervous wreck.

· 369 ·

Volunteer at your local public radio
station and find out how programs
are actually produced.

· 370 ·

Shop the antique fairs for old-fashioned
pillowcases with luscious embroidered,
eyelet, or lace edging.

· 371 ·

Spend a day at the races.

· 372 ·
Spend a night at the opera.

· 373 ·
Organize your desk drawers.

· 374 ·
Buy next year's calendar in October
and be ready for the new year.

· 375 ·
Travel to see a world-class
tennis tournament.

· 376 ·
Browse in one of the smaller bookstores:
an independent general bookstore,
specialty bookstore, used book store,
rare book store.

· 377 ·
Take belly dancing lessons.

· 378 ·

Give yourself a bouquet of sweet peas.

· 379 ·

Get a new air conditioner.

✳ *Clear the junk out of the attic.*

✳ *Don't clear the junk out of the attic.*

· 382 ·

Pick up a quart container of hearty chicken
soup and a couple of fresh rolls on your
way home. Hunker down in your favorite
chair and have a cozy dinner.

· 383 ·

Read a whole book of the cartoons
of your favorite cartoonist and laugh
until your stomach hurts.

· 384 ·

Pamper your houseplants: Feed them
and water them, keep their
leaves and pots clean, cut
them back when necessary.

· 385 ·

Tell the telephone pollster that you're not
in the mood for answering questions.

· 386 ·

Buy a lottery ticket once a week.

· 387 ·

Record your grandparents' stories on
tape, so you'll always have them.

· 388 ·

Put self-stick flags on your
favorite cookbook recipes, so you'll
be able to find them instantly.

· 389 ·

Clear the unwanted or useless information
out of your computer files.

· 390 ·

Stop using soup cans for weights.
Get a good pair of dumbbells.

· 391 ·

Don't cook anything for the potluck supper.
Buy something instead.

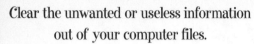

❀ Give yourself a break:
Don't worry about the things you didn't have
time to do today. You'll do them tomorrow—
or maybe they didn't really need doing . . .

· 393 ·

Hang a wind chime on the porch.

· 394 ·

Take a watercolor painting class.

· 395 ·

Take a course on interior decorating.

· 396 ·

Commission a handmade sweater
from an expert knitter.

· 397 ·

Throw out or give away those old
neckties that make your mate look
out of date and out of style.

· 398 ·

Plan the trip of your dreams. Decide where,
when, and how to get there. Read about your
destination and get travel brochures. Start a
savings account especially for the trip.

· 399 ·

Watch the moon and planets through
a telescope. Be mindful of how
large your universe is.

· 400 ·

Make a list of the things you like about yourself. Be honest. And don't show the list to anyone else—it's your secret.

· 401 ·

Buy yourself one big bag of Hershey's Kisses and another of Hugs.

· 402 ·

Have the strolling musicians play your favorite song.

· 403 ·

Call the Dial-a-Joke line.

· 404 ·

Remain friendly with your ex.

· 405 ·

Change your style of dress to reflect your new circumstances.

· 406 ·

Plant a rose garden, a lilac bush, a honeysuckle vine, a wall of morning glories, a bed of pansies.

· 407 ·

Make love outdoors.

· 408 ·

Get enough sleep.

· 409 ·

Keep a little snack in your handbag for low-energy moments.

· 410 ·

Keep an extra pair of pantyhose in your desk drawer at work.

· 411 ·

Plan your outfits for the coming week,
so you don't have to think about
them in the morning.

· 412 ·

Wear your lucky jewelry
whenever you're heading
for a tough situation.

· 413 ·

Ask a friend to meet you right
after a stressful event—driver's test,
job interview, bar exam.

❀ *Do yourself a favor:*
Pay no attention to people who
discourage you from trying
new things, making progress,
changing your life.

· 415 ·

Make a special trip to another city
to see an art show, play, or musical
with a limited engagement.

· 416 ·

Read a few of the Great American Novels
you missed in high school: *Death Comes
for the Archbishop* by Willa Cather,
The Great Gatsby by F. Scott Fitzgerald,
The Grapes of Wrath by John Steinbeck,
Franny and Zooey by J. D. Salinger.

· 417 ·

Buy really good wine for a change.

· 418 ·

Feast on a black Périgord truffle
from France or a white Alba
truffle from Italy.

· 419 ·

Make a list of restaurants
you want to try and check
them off as you go to them.

· 420 ·

Start a file of mean, nasty letters you'll never
send: to the old high school friend who
snubbed you, the salesperson who gave you
a hard time, the relative who insulted you,
the personnel manager who didn't hire you.

· 421 ·

Take a course in public speaking.

· 422 ·

Learn to type. (Even CEOs know
how to type.)

· 423 ·

Improve your work life with
all-new folders for your files.

· 424 ·

Become a mentor.

· 425 ·

Have your colors done.

· 426 ·

Go on a diet but *don't tell anyone*,
even your best friend. If no one knows,
no one will scold you when you have a
temporary setback, or sabotage you by
trying to make you eat.

· 427 ·

Frequent a really great salad bar.

· 428 ·

Treat yourself to an espresso
maker and a set of those little
white espresso cups.

· 429 ·

Instead of plain white paper or
cloth napkins, use pretty
colored or patterned ones.

· 430 ·

Instead of plain checks for your checkbook,
next time order fancy ones.

· 431 ·

Duplicate your weekly grocery list at
a copy shop, so you don't have to write out
the same items fifty-two times a year.

· 432 ·

Have the groceries delivered.

· 433 ·

Have the Sunday paper delivered.

· 434 ·

Buy a toaster oven.

· 435 ·

Invite friends for a continental breakfast:
coffee, tea, hot rolls and muffins,
jam, and fruit served from a sideboard
or the kitchen counter.

· 436 ·

Mooch around the house doing
nothing, in the oldest, softest jeans
and shirt you own.

· 437 ·

Ignore your telephone messages
for a couple of days.

· 438 ·

If you don't like talking on the phone,
make calls when you *know* you'll
get the answering machine.

❀ *Give yourself a break:*
Think for yourself. Live your own life,
not your mother's, your sister's,
or your best friend's.

· 440 ·

Cave in and buy those sensational
tooled, stitched cowboy boots you've
been hankering after.

· 441 ·

Make a ceremony of purchasing
your first cashmere sweater.

· 442 ·

If you can't have a whole room of your own,
carve out a space in a corner of another
room. Put up a screen, a curtain, or
even a tent to get some privacy.

· 443 ·

Show off your diplomas and awards
in good-looking frames.

· 444 ·

Take your birthday off from work.

· 445 ·

Take a sick day when you're not sick.

· 446 ·

Stay in bed when you have the flu.

· 447 ·

Administer a daily dose of laughter:
Keep up with "Sally Forth," "For Better
or for Worse," and "Cathy."

· 448 ·

Stock up on your favorite munchies.

· 449 ·

Hire a trainer to teach your
dog how to behave.

· 450 ·

Build an extra bathroom so you
don't have to share.

· 451 ·

String Japanese
lanterns across the backyard.

· 452 ·

Buy yourself an exquisite new chess set.

· 453 ·

Write a letter to the editor about that issue
with which you're vitally concerned.

· 454 ·

Visit the San Diego Wild Animal Park.

· 455 ·
Try one of those disposable cameras
that takes panoramic pictures.

· 456 ·
Arrange your CDs or your books according
to how you feel about them, starting with
your favorite in the top left corner and
working across and down.

· 457 ·
Take a class to learn to cook dishes
from a cuisine you love: Italian, French,
Chinese, Mexican, Thai, Indian.

· 458 ·
Have someone clean your oven for you.

· 459 ·
Schedule a pleasurable activity
right after a difficult one.

· 460 ·

When you receive a call from someone you don't want to talk to, set your oven timer for five minutes. Put it near the phone, so your caller hears it when it buzzes or beeps. Say, "Oops, sorry, have to go now," and hang up.

· 461 ·

Get an unlisted phone number.

· 462 ·

Get a cellular phone.

· 463 ·

Get a second phone line.

· 464 ·

Get a bigger refrigerator.

· 465 ·

Get a bigger bed.

· 466 ·

Lead someone down the primrose path.

· 467 ·

Practice safe sex.

· 468 ·

Run cold water over your wrists and inside
your elbows for a quick refresher.

· 469 ·

Cool off with a mini-size
personal fan on your desk.

· 470 ·

Keep a bottle of water in the fridge
for icy-cold thirst quenching.

· 471 ·

Put on your galoshes before you
go out in the rain.

· 472 ·

Tuck a tissue or two into the pocket of each
of your jackets and coats, so you'll always
have a hankie when you need it.

· 473 ·

Put off till tomorrow whatever you
planned to do today.

· 474 ·

Stash a log of homemade refrigerator cookie
dough in the freezer. Slice and bake for a
quick treat any time you get the munchies.

❀ *Do yourself a favor:*

If you're doing more than your
share, speak up.

· 476 ·

Instead of going straight home after work,
go out and have fun with your friends.

· 477 ·

Treat yourself to the microscope you
always wanted when you were a kid.

· 478 ·

Be good to yourself by being good to
others. When you replace appliances,
computers, audio or video equipment,
or even your car, take the time to donate
the older model to a charity.

· 479 ·

Go to a scary movie at midnight,
but don't go alone.

· 480 ·

Drop your clothes wherever you take
them off, and don't think about picking
them up until tomorrow.

· 481 ·

Drape your bathrobe over the foot
of the bed, so you can grab it the
minute you get up.

· 482 ·

Drink your café au lait from
a thick ceramic bowl.

· 483 ·

Drink your tea from a
delicate china cup.

· 484 ·

Eat glazed doughnuts.

· 485 ·

Quit the job you hate and
find one you love—or at least
find one you like.

· 486 ·

Cancel a date you're dreading:
dinner with an old high school boyfriend,
tea with Great-aunt Elizabeth, lunch
with an acquaintance who's always
a tiny bit nasty to you.

· 487 ·

Tear your to-do list in half. Save the
other half for next week.

· 488 ·

Take your book and your sunglasses and
settle down at a sidewalk café for an
afternoon of reading and people-watching.
If you can do it in a foreign country,
so much the better!

· 489 ·

Treat yourself to a whole book
of crossword puzzles.

· 490 ·

Ask for paper bags instead of plastic
at the supermarket.

· 491 ·

Stop clipping grocery coupons
for one month.

· 492 ·

Throw out your junk mail
without reading it.

· 493 ·

Read everything ever written by
your favorite author.

· 494 ·

Have your beloved-but-completely-worn-out
handbag copied by a leather craftsperson.

· 495 ·
Have your family heirlooms
appraised by an expert.

· 496 ·
Visit the museums of the Smithsonian
Institution in Washington, D.C.

· 497 ·
Fly a kite.

· 498 ·
Grow an orchid.

· 499 ·
Make a sand castle.

Give yourself a break:
Let your children sleep in their
sleeping bags. Zip them up and
the beds are made.

· 501 ·
Pick wild blackberries.

· 502 ·
Make an old-fashioned grilled
cheese sandwich.

· 503 ·
Have a chocolate feast:
chocolate éclairs, chocolate mousse,
chocolate pudding, chocolate brownies,
chocolate cookies, chocolate ice cream.

· 504 ·
Try on hats. Lots of hats.

· 505 ·
Throw yourself a
birthday party, so you
can get plenty
of presents.

· 506 ·

Send your sheets and towels
to the local laundry instead of
doing them yourself.

· 507 ·

At the January white sales, pick up
a couple dozen new facecloths.
Use a fresh one every day.

· 508 ·

Work up a righteous sweat
playing tennis all day.

· 509 ·

Watch while everyone else works up
a sweat playing tennis all day.

· 510 ·

Look at your city from a stranger's point
of view. Isn't it a great place?

· 511 ·

Fill in for your mother, your sister,
your boss for a day—and then be overjoyed
to return to your own life.

· 512 ·

Refinish a beautiful piece of (nonantique!)
furniture—slowly, carefully, lovingly.

· 513 ·

Use cloth napkins for the pleasure of it.

· 514 ·

Take a stretch limo at least once in your life.

· 515 ·

Have a split of champagne with your dinner.

· 516 ·

Buy an inexpensive set of twenty-four
wineglasses to use for parties.

· 517 ·

On the spur of the moment,
call a friend and toddle off for a great
lunch and an afternoon of shopping.

· 518 ·

Leave your bags and packages in the
checkroom of the department store, so
you can enjoy burden-free shopping.

· 519 ·

Think about where you're going.
Is it where you want to go? Allow yourself
to contemplate other possibilities
and how to achieve them.

· 520 ·

Eat as much guacamole and
tortilla chips as you want.

· 521 ·

Make fresh pesto in summer,
when basil flourishes.

· 522 ·

Make extra pesto, freeze it in small
Ziploc bags, and savor it all winter.

· 523 ·

Spend an afternoon swinging
lazily in a hammock.

· 524 ·

Find time for all the movies you want to see.

* Attend your high school
  reunion.

* Don't attend your high
  school reunion.

· 527 ·

Request your favorite song on
a local radio station.

· 528 ·

Don't miss your favorite sitcom
or cop show for anything.

· 529 ·

Get in bed an hour early every night for
a week. Use the extra hour for reading,
knitting, mending, writing a letter, listening
to the radio, watching TV—or even sleeping.

· 530 ·

Join a carpool, so you don't have
to do all the driving.

· 531 ·

Give away all the pots, pans,
and dishes you never use.

· 532 ·

If you can't remember a thing,
get a small memo recorder.

· 533 ·

Order a stamper with your
name and address on it.

· 534 ·

Label your storage boxes.

· 535 ·

Go through your files and toss out
all the obsolete papers.

· 536 ·

Take a tour boat around an island,
up a river, across a bay. Throw
your troubles to the wind.

· 537 ·

If you're feeling as if you haven't come a
long way, baby, visit the National Women's
Hall of Fame in Seneca Falls, New York.

 Give yourself a break:
Remember that it's not necessary
to win every battle. Sometimes it's
kinder to *yourself* to walk away
gracefully from a fight.

· 539 ·

Eat a nutritious, balanced diet.

· 540 ·

Take vitamins.

· 541 ·

Spend some time in a tub
with a Jacuzzi.

· 542 ·

Have a scalp massage.

· 543 ·

Build something amazing with Legos.

· 544 ·

On a sultry summer day, have your kids
spray you with the garden hose.

· 545 ·

Turn on the air conditioning
whenever you feel like it.

· 546 ·

Plant a window box full of begonias,
geraniums, or petunias.

· 547 ·

If you have a boring chore to do, break it up
into one-hour units of work, interspersed
with one-hour units of fun.

❀ *Do yourself a favor:*
Try to have patience. Whatever it is you're
impatient about may take an hour, a day,
or even a week to resolve itself.

· 549 ·
Figure out what (or who) gives you
comfort and then do your best to keep it
(or them) in your life.

· 550 ·
Look at your baby pictures and
see how cute you were.

· 551 ·
Take your daughter to work with you. Let
her see how terrific you are at your job.

· 552 ·
Shop in small stores where there are no
crowds and you get wonderful personal
attention from the sales staff.

· 553 ·

Change the mood of your bedroom
with a new bedspread in a wonderful
fabric—velvet, satin, patchwork,
chenille, corduroy, lace, fake fur.

· 554 ·

Take an art appreciation
course at a museum.

· 555 ·

Keep your desk cleared off
for a whole week.

· 556 ·

Have enough bookshelves for your books.

· 557 ·

Build a glassed-in conservatory bay
onto one of your bedroom windows,
and fill it with blooming plants.

· 558 ·
Hire someone to cut the grass.

· 559 ·
Take a vacation with your best friend.

· 560 ·
Let your partner buy you a present when
you're out shopping together.

· 561 ·
See an experimental theater piece to prove
to yourself how daring you are.

· 562 ·
Upgrade your technology: Go on-line.
Get E-mail. Add memory. Consider buying a
new computer that really meets your needs.

· 563 ·
Paint your fingernails an outrageous color.

· 564 ·

Yell yourself silly at a basketball game.

· 565 ·

Learn to ski—downhill or cross-country.

· 566 ·

Buy a pair of energizing, supercomfortable
workout or running shoes.

· 567 ·

Pamper your waistline: Switch from ice
cream to sorbet.

· 568 ·

Stop at a farm stand and buy a
melon still warm from the field.
Sit at the side of the road, slice the
melon, and eat it right away.

· 569 ·

Hang a cluster of gorgeously colored
Indian corn on your door to welcome
you home on an autumn day.

· 570 ·

Line your bureau drawers
with beautiful paper.

· 571 ·

Be sure to have a comfortable
armchair or sofa in
your home office.

· 572 ·

Lie on the floor and put your feet
up on the bed. Close your eyes,
breathe, and relax.

· 573 ·

Play catnip games with your pussycat.

· 574 ·

Get tickets to a mesmerizing magic show.

· 575 ·

Do a great big jigsaw puzzle.

· 576 ·

Learn to use chopsticks.

· 577 ·

Try an electric toothbrush.

✳ *Stop biting your nails.*

✳ *Bite your nails if you want to.*

· 580 ·

Take an assertiveness training class.

· 581 ·

Decline to be a chaperone at the prom.

· 582 ·

If you've always hated your name, change it.

· 583 ·

Beg off at least one out of every
four family events.

 Give yourself a break:
Stop cleaning up after your
a) spouse
b) children
c) pets
d) all of the above

· 585 ·

Go to a jewelry store and try on fancy
earrings just for the fun of it.

· 586 ·

Buy yourself a chic basic black dress
and wear it with pearls.

· 587 ·

Pamper yourself with *blue*:
Wedgwood china, blue suede shoes,
cobalt glass bottles on your windowsill,
blueberry pie, a bouquet of cornflowers,
a blue denim jacket, sapphires.

· 588 ·

Pamper yourself with *red*:
shiny apples, scarlet zinnias and
dahlias, rubies, beaujolais nouveau,
red satin ribbons, red Keds, hand-knit
red mittens, terra-cotta tiles.

· 589 ·

Pamper yourself with *yellow*:
sweet corn, a yellow sundress, golden
raisins, fresh lemons, primroses and
daffodils, topazes, a yellow rain slicker.

· 590 ·

Pamper yourself with *green*:
fresh herbs, a freshly mowed lawn,
juicy olives, branches of holly and pine,
pistachio ice cream, a great pool table,
mint frosting, emeralds.

· 591 ·

Pamper yourself with *pink*:
roses, cotton candy, blush wine, fresh
salmon, pink furry slippers, a pink satin
nightgown, a strawberry smoothie, pink
lightbulbs, cherry nail polish.

· 592 ·

Pamper yourself with *violet*:
lilacs and freesia, amethysts,
plum jam, grapes growing
in an arbor, lavender
soap, purple heather.

· 593 ·

Pamper yourself with *orange*: fresh
pumpkin, ripe cantaloupe, amber beads,
carrot cake, candy corn, pots of marigolds,
sharp Cheddar cheese, glacé apricots,
a miniature orange tree.

· 594 ·

Plant an herb garden near your kitchen,
or in pots on a sunny windowsill.

· 595 ·

Wallow in romance novels for a month.

· 596 ·

Dance cheek-to-cheek with your lover.

· 597 ·

Spend an afternoon thinking lofty
thoughts at the Air and Space Museum
in Washington, D.C.

Don't postpone your dreams.

Book an afternoon on a small sailboat.
Feel the wind and the spray
and the speed, but don't
do any of the work.

Get a sleek chrome cocktail shaker for
making martinis—and then make some.

Treat yourself to a custom-made suit.

Have your foundation makeup or
powder custom-made.

Let your nails grow.

· 604 ·

Eat a tin of caviar.

· 605 ·

Buy several servings of lasagna from
your favorite Italian restaurant.
Wrap and freeze for last-minute dinners.

· 606 ·

Use paper plates and napkins, so you don't
have to wash any dishes.

· 607 ·

Buy paper towels by the eight-pack.
You'll always have a roll handy.

· 608 ·

Require your kids to do whatever household
chores they're capable of. And no excuses.

· 609 ·

Take your shirts to a laundry service.

· 610 ·

Hire a plumber to fix the leaks.

* *Read books about how to
get organized.*

* *Don't read books about
how to get organized.*

· 613 ·

Enjoy every moment of the day.

· 614 ·

Take singing lessons.

· 615 ·

Get a tarot reading.

· 616 ·

Go to a polka party.

· 617 ·

Learn to stand on your head.

· 618 ·

Take a long bike ride into the country
or to a part of town unfamiliar to you.
Explore as if you were ten years old.

· 619 ·

Spend an afternoon in bed, surrounded
by a tray of tasty food, books and
magazines, a radio, the remote control,
your crocheting, your pet.

· 620 ·

If a million problems and things-to-do are
spinning around in your head and keeping
you from falling asleep, get up and write
them down. Now put the list away and
forget about it till morning.

· 621 ·

Let your hair dry in the sun.

· 622 ·

Squeeze fresh grapefruit juice into
your vodka-on-the-rocks.

· 623 ·

Feel free to hug your nearest and dearest
at any time. Teach them to hug back.

· 624 ·

Cook up a big pot of homemade
lentil or pea soup.

· 625 ·

Buy yourself a heart-shaped,
red satin box of assorted
chocolates.

· 626 ·

Carry your portable phone
around the house with you, so
you don't miss any calls.

· 627 ·

Read your favorite columnist
in the paper every day.

· 628 ·

Read the diaries of famous people.
Discover that they did some of the
same things you do.

· 629 ·

Buy a painting you love.

· 630 ·

Collect folk art.

· 631 ·

Go horseback riding on a
clear autumn day.

· 632 ·

Fall down laughing at tapes or
CDs of stand-up comedy routines.

· 633 ·

Watch a pair of videos—the original and
the new version: *An Affair to Remember*
and *Sleepless in Seattle, Cape Fear,
A Star Is Born, La Cage aux Folles* and
The Birdcage, Psycho, Little Women.

· 634 ·

Pin a corsage of violets to your coat.

· 635 ·

Wear a jaunty beret.

· 636 ·

Visit an artist's studio on an
"open studio" day.

· 637 ·

Build yourself a beautiful
workbench with room for all your
tools and equipment.

· 638 ·

Construct a storage wall, using
modular units arranged according
to your own specific needs.

· 639 ·

Paint your ceiling sky blue.

· 640 ·

Install dimmer switches in the
dining room, bedroom, and bath.

· 641 ·

Get a self-defrosting refrigerator.

· 642 ·

Stock your pantry with extra
staples: flour, sugar, rice, pasta,
tomato sauce, and others.

· 643 ·

Stock up on a few simple gifts
(games for kids, T-shirts or boxes of pretty
notecards for grown-ups), so you don't have
to do a last-minute dash when you
unexpectedly need a present.

 Give yourself a break:
Let your fingers do the walking.
Call before you shop.

· 645 ·

Visit friends in another city.

· 646 ·

Invite friends from another
city to visit you.

· 647 ·

Take the Sunday paper and a
breakfast picnic to the park.

· 648 ·

Let the garden go to weeds
for a week or two.

· 649 ·

Dust yourself with deliciously scented
floral bath powder—gardenia, lily of
the valley, jasmine, carnation.

· 650 ·

Wrap up in layers of soft sweaters.

· 651 ·

Wear an ankle bracelet.

· 652 ·

Indulge in (safe) fantasies with your lover.

· 653 ·

Order the tasting menu at
a fabulous restaurant.

· 654 ·

Dance all night and stroll home at dawn.

· 655 ·

Ride a ferry back and forth at
least twice without getting off.

· 656 ·

If you travel a lot, buy a good travel wallet
that will hold everything: passport, tickets,
itinerary, hotel confirmation, and so on.

· 657 ·

Buy a hot novel or mystery to keep you
enthralled during a long plane trip.

· 658 ·

Borrow an RV and hit the
road for a weekend.

· 659 ·

Treat yourself to a pair of binoculars.

· 660 ·

Take a flying lesson.

· 661 ·

Get an exercise bike.

· 662 ·

Do not obsess about the
condition of your thighs.

· 663 ·

Do not obsess about the
size of your breasts.

· 664 ·

Do not obsess about the
width of your hips.

· 665 ·

Do not obsess about wrinkles. You have
earned them honorably by hanging in there
and getting to be whatever age you are.

· 666 ·

Read novels
by women.

· 667 ·

Remind a short-tempered,
impatient, insensitive young person
that he or she will be older someday too.

· 668 ·

Decide to be less passive, and start
taking small steps toward a different
way of living—even if the people
around you don't like it.

· 669 ·

Sign up for a class that focuses on
breathing techniques, relaxation,
and stress management.

· 670 ·

If you're having trouble balancing work
and family, explore the possibilities of
flextime. It just might work for you.

· 671 ·

Throw away clothes that
are worn out and make you look
like a bag lady.

· 672 ·

Buy new accessories to go with
your favorite suit or dress.

· 673 ·

Find a bra that fits you perfectly
and buy three.

· 674 ·

Wear socks to bed.

· 675 ·

Play card games to relax:
solitaire, gin rummy, canasta.

· 676 ·

Have a corned beef on rye with Russian
dressing, and a cream soda to go with it.

· 677 ·

Sit where *you* want to sit
in the movie theater.

· 678 ·

Renew your library card and take out
the maximum number of books.

· 679 ·

Taste the free samples at a
gourmet food shop.

❋ *Give yourself a break:*
Stop worrying about what other
people will think.

· 681 ·

Lose yourself—staring at the flames, gazing at the waves, listening to music, kneading bread, swinging in a hammock.

· 682 ·

Do *not* read a scary or upsetting book before bed.

· 683 ·

Twist Oreos apart and eat only the frosted halves. Don't forget the milk.

· 684 ·

Make cinnamon toast.

· 685 ·

Crochet a soft afghan that matches your couch, so you can nap in style.

· 686 ·

Try flannel sheets.

· 687 ·

Ditch those ratty old blankets and
buy soft, warm new ones.

· 688 ·

Divest yourself of those threadbare,
frayed towels. Get new ones in a color
you've always wanted—kiwi or berry,
periwinkle or champagne.

· 689 ·

Buy a whole case of whatever bottled
beverage you love to drink: wine, beer,
juice, iced tea, spring water.

· 690 ·

Get a real ice bucket.

· 691 ·

Welcome spring
with a pot of
hyacinths or narcissi.

· 692 ·

Stock up on lightbulbs, soap,
and toilet paper.

· 693 ·

Can't find the twist-ties?
Switch to Ziploc bags.

· 694 ·

Hire a dog-walker.

· 695 ·

Put in a pet door, so you're
not at the mercy of
your animal.

❀ *Do yourself a favor:*
You don't have to go to *every* game
your children play in. And you don't
have to feel guilty about it, either.

· 697 ·

Ask your grandparents to tell you
the worst stuff your parents did when
they were young. Think about those
stories when your mom and dad
give you a hard time.

· 698 ·

Go to a drive-in movie, for old time's sake.

· 699 ·

Go to a family-style community supper
at a church, firehouse, or school.

· 700 ·

Make a pot of thick, delicious
chili with beans.

· 701 ·

Make a pot of thick, delicious
chili without beans.

· 702 ·

Have as many barbecued
spareribs as you want.

· 703 ·

Play board games: Monopoly,
Trivial Pursuit, Scrabble, Clue,
Chinese checkers, Parcheesi.

❋ *Give yourself a break:*
Get away from your problems
for a whole day. Drive to a nearby city,
spend eight hours at the mall, go to
the beach—do whatever it takes to
stay *out of touch* for the day.

· 705 ·

If big department stores
give you anxiety attacks,
keep out of them.

· 706 ·

If you hate shopping, take a
shopping-maven friend along and
let her help you get what you need.
Invite her to lunch to thank her.

· 707 ·

Stop wearing high heels.

· 708 ·

Do *not* try to be as thin as a model.

❀ *Do yourself a favor:*

Tell the imaginary critics (the ones
standing at your shoulder, disapproving of
everything you do) to get lost for good.

· 710 ·

Look through a kaleidoscope and
enjoy the colorful, changing image
in the little round glass.

· 711 ·

Have someone scratch your back.

· 712 ·

Buy a waterproof pillow for your bath, and
one of those trays that bridge the tub—to
hold your cool drink (or glass of wine) and
your book or magazine. Luxuriate.

· 713 ·

Take swimming lessons to
improve your stroke.

· 714 ·

Dig a little pond in front or back of your
house, and make a water garden.

· 715 ·

Find a great (and reliable) fish store.

· 716 ·
Join (or start) a bridge club.

· 717 ·
Take one of your grandchildren on a trip.

· 718 ·
Play silly word games—such as "I Packed
My Grandmother's Suitcase" and "Twenty
Questions"—with a group of friends.

· 719 ·
Attend a folk, rock, or jazz festival.

· 720 ·
Get headphones, in order to listen
to your favorite CDs without getting
complaints from *anyone*.

· 721 ·
Stock up on extra batteries, so you'll
have them when you need them.

· 722 ·

Talk to the television as
much as you want.

· 723 ·

Pick up a jar of that soapy, slippery
bubble stuff and blow bubbles.

· 724 ·

Have a pillow fight.

· 725 ·

Keep popping the sticks of gum into your
mouth, so the flavor never goes away.

· 726 ·

Invest in a super-duper new toothbrush.

* *Nosh between meals.*

* *Don't nosh between meals.*

· 729 ·

Pack a delicious picnic lunch next
time you travel, so you don't have to
eat the airline meal, the café car food,
or the rest-stop snacks.

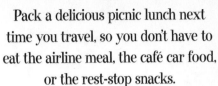

· 730 ·

Visit the Baseball Hall of Fame
in Cooperstown, New York.

· 731 ·

Save time: Write postcards
instead of letters.

· 732 ·

Use self-adhesive stamps.

· 733 ·

Get a new address book.

· 734 ·

Make unpleasant phone calls early,
and follow them up *immediately* with
cozy calls to good friends.

· 735 ·

Whether you're a parent, a teacher,
a secretary, a lawyer, or a painter,
you need community. Get out there
and find like-minded colleagues.

· 736 ·

Take part in a light opera or operetta, even
if you only make it into the chorus.

· 737 ·

Go roller skating at an old-fashioned rink
with piped-in skating music.

· 738 ·

Prepare hot mulled cider from the fresh
cider you buy at a farm stand.

· 739 ·

Visit Lancaster County, Pennsylvania,
and treat yourself to lots of yummy
Pennsylvania Dutch relishes and preserves.

· 740 ·

Get in touch with your roots:
Take a trip to the country or city your
family originally came from.

· 741 ·

Videotape the important
events in your life.

· 742 ·

When you throw a party, hire help:
kitchen minder, waitstaff, bartender.

· 743 ·

Buy shrimp already
shelled and cleaned.

· 744 ·

Order desserts by mail—anything from
pound cake to chocolates.

· 745 ·

Eat chocolate-covered pretzels.

· 746 ·

Resolve not to cook for a week.
Or a month. Or a year.

 Give yourself a break:
There's no law that says you must serve as
scoutmaster, block association president,
PTA treasurer, or anything else. Take on
only what you have time and energy to do.

· 748 ·

If you love having overnight guests
but you have no guest room,
invest in a sleep sofa.

· 749 ·

If you hate having overnight guests,
decline politely.

· 750 ·

Get comfortable in big,
slouchy socks and a big,
soft sweatshirt.

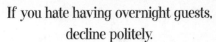

· 751 ·

Turn your bedroom into a refuge
from the day's stresses.

· 752 ·

Think of your garden as an
extension of your wardrobe.
Fill it with your favorite
colors and shapes.

· 753 ·

Spend an afternoon roaming around
with your camera, taking interesting
shots of people (not your family)
and places (not your home).

· 754 ·

Take advantage of opportunities
when they occur.

· 755 ·

Start fresh: fresh notebook,
fresh towels, fresh strawberries,
fresh air.

· 756 ·

Alter your look (hairstyle, makeup,
clothes) as you get older.

· 757 ·

Go into action at the first
sign of middle-age spread.

❀ *Do yourself a favor:*
Tell your partner what's bothering you.

· 759 ·

Rub sore muscles with a pain-relieving
liquid or gel.

· 760 ·

Rest your tired head on an herbal
therapy pillow—support for your neck
plus the soothing scent of chamomile,
lavender, or other herbs.

· 761 ·

Close your bedroom door and do fifteen
minutes of really good stretches, from
your neck down to your toes.

· 762 ·

Buy a new bathing suit to go with
your new buff body.

· 763 ·

Quit the volunteer work you dislike, and
find some volunteer work you love.

· 764 ·

Finish your degree—high school, trade
school, college, or grad school.

· 765 ·

Have beautiful business cards
printed up for yourself.

· 766 ·

Purchase a debit phone card,
so you can make calls from a
telephone booth without having
to search for change.

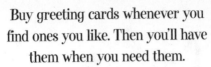

· 767 ·

Buy greeting cards whenever you
find ones you like. Then you'll have
them when you need them.

· 768 ·

Read a *Life* magazine from the
year you were born.

· 769 ·

Let your mother tell you what an
adorable baby you were.

· 770 ·

Let your best pal tell you what
a fantastic friend you are.

· 771 ·

Let your mate tell you how smart
and gorgeous you are.

· 772 ·

Have your portrait painted.

· 773 ·

Keep a sense of humor about life.

· 774 ·

Get mad *and* get even.

· 775 ·

Take a ceramics class and
learn to throw pots.

· 776 ·

Get rid of all your houseplants.

· 777 ·

Wean the baby.

· 778 ·

Swear off frozen vegetables.

· 779 ·

Pet a dolphin.

❋ *Give yourself a break:*
Cry in public. Someone will comfort you.

· 781 ·

Treat yourself to soft ice cream
in a waffle cone, dipped in
chocolate topping.

· 782 ·

Eat as many plump,
dark cherries as you want.

· 783 ·

Dine at a four-star restaurant.

· 784 ·

Set your porch light on a timer, and come
home to a welcoming house.

· 785 ·

Establish a Red Alert signal with
your partner (such as tapping your
nose or pulling your earlobe), so he
can rescue you from a bad social
situation—a boring relative, a hostile
drunk, an offensive guest.

· 786 ·

Put together a survival kit for short-term
power failures: flashlights, candles, battery-
operated radio, deck of cards, board games.
Stash it in an easy-to-reach spot.

· 787 ·

Treat yourself to a fancy pocketknife
with lots of blades and gadgets.

· 788 ·

Wear a helmet when you're
riding your bike.

· 789 ·

Buy an extra umbrella. The day will
surely come when you leave yours
in a restaurant or taxi and need one
the very next morning.

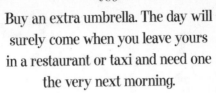

❀ *Do yourself a favor:*
Store your valuables and important
papers in a safety deposit box.

· 791 ·

Insist that your partner slow down if his
driving speed is scaring the pants off you.

· 792 ·

Meet your blind date in a public place.
Never take chances with your own safety.

· 793 ·

Never open the door to a stranger until
you've verified his identity.

· 794 ·

Install a reliable security system.

· 795 ·

Ask your partner to get out of
bed and check the scary noise you
hear in the middle of the night.

· 796 ·

Keep a flashlight in the drawer of your
night table. Extra batteries too.

· 797 ·

Learn to relax with videos on stress
management, massage techniques,
or stretching exercises. All in the
privacy of your own home.

· 798 ·

At the end of the day, kick back
and have an icy-cold beer.

· 799 ·

Look through a book of "Far Side" cartoons
and don't worry about what they mean.

· 800 ·

Get yourself a good dictionary
and a good thesaurus.

· 801 ·

Express yourself: Write a letter to the
author of a book you loved reading.

· 802 ·

Get tickets to that show you've
been dying to see.

· 803 ·

Treat yourself to a box set of your favorite
classics: Frank Sinatra, Aretha Franklin,
Tony Bennett, Duke Ellington, Cole Porter,
Rodgers and Hart, Ray Charles, Peggy Lee.

· 804 ·

If you can't afford a good audio system,
get a high-quality boom box instead.

· 805 ·

Ban television for a night, a week,
a month, or a year.

· 806 ·

Put a radio in every room,
for your listening pleasure.

· 807 ·

Tune in to *Fresh Air*, with host Terry Gross,
on your local public radio station.

· 808 ·

Sit in a patch of sunlight in
a glade in the woods. Lean your
back against a sturdy tree trunk
and let your mind wander.

· 809 ·
Use sunblock.

· 810 ·
Pick up a bright straw tote
for summer.

· 811 ·
Wear an armful of bangle bracelets.

· 812 ·
Take two showers on a sticky,
humid day.

· 813 ·
Powder your toes.

· 814 ·
Sunburned? Take a cool bath in
which you've dissolved a quarter of
a cup of baking soda.

· 815 ·

In hot weather, keep your cologne,
lipstick, and hand cream in the refrigerator.
They'll be a pleasure to use.

· 816 ·

Just this once, don't clean the
bathtub after your bath.

· 817 ·

Serve breakfast orange juice
in wineglasses.

· 818 ·

Eat a great cinnamon-raisin sticky bun.

· 819 ·

Slice a juicy fresh peach
(preferably warm from the sun),
drown it in cream, and eat immediately.

· 820 ·

Put clean sheets on the bed
whenever you feel like it.

· 821 ·

Get an electric can opener.

· 822 ·

Make a list of ten things that would
make you feel more secure—
and try to make them happen.

· 823 ·

If you could live in another part of town,
what area would you choose? Go look at
apartments. Maybe you *can* live over there.

· 824 ·

Have three outfits, complete with
accessories and shoes, that will get
you through any occasion.

· 825 ·

On a cold night, make Irish coffee:
strong coffee, Irish whiskey, a bit of sugar,
and a dollop of whipped cream.

· 826 ·

Go on a trip to
see wild animals
in the wild.

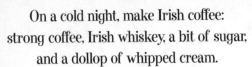

· 827 ·

Read a sexy book.

· 828 ·

Have a real Coke instead
of a diet Coke.

Give yourself a break:
Don't let small snits turn into big fights.
Find out what the problem is
and deal with it *now.*

· 830 ·

Take speech lessons to develop
a beautiful speaking voice.

· 831 ·

Treat yourself to party food on an
ordinary day: cheese sticks, canapés, mixed
nuts, anchovy-stuffed olives, Camembert,
salmon roe, smoked oysters.

· 832 ·

If you've always wanted to direct, get
yourself a video recorder and go for it.

· 833 ·

Visit Point Reyes National Seashore,
north of San Francisco, California.

· 834 ·

Take out the old family photo
album and tell stories about the
pictures, for hours on end.

· 835 ·

Have your favorite poster, painting,
or print framed. Hang it where
you can see it often.

· 836 ·

When your apartment is
crowded with too much furniture
and too many objects, rent storage
space and clear it out.

· 837 ·

If you don't want to go to the party
(or any other event), don't go.

· 838 ·

Turn your attic into the a) workroom,
b) office, c) bedroom, or
d) playroom you've always wanted.

· 839 ·

Build a porch or deck onto
your bedroom.

· 840 ·

Build a gazebo in your backyard.

· 841 ·

Cook all your dinners outside
on a gas grill for at least a week.
No pots and pans to clean!

· 842 ·

Get a wheely cart for transporting
food, drinks, and tableware out to the patio
or yard, so you can do it all in one trip.

· 843 ·

Give a huge party that mixes
guests of different ages,
sexes, races, ethnicities.

· 844 ·

Tune into the world: Buy yourself
one of the new, easy-to-use
shortwave radios.

✳ *Go to a blockbuster movie.*

✳ *Boycott a blockbuster movie.*

· 847 ·

Have a mad shopping spree
in a factory outlet store.

· 848 ·

Fall in love with an antique car, buy it,
and restore it to its former glory.

· 849 ·

Fall in love with an old house,
buy it, and restore it to
its former glory.

· 850 ·

Try a sport you think you'd be
good at but haven't given a chance:
lacrosse, bowling, golf, scuba
diving, tennis, or climbing.

· 851 ·

Defy gravity: Jump on a trampoline.

· 852 ·

Go skinny-dipping with your beloved.

· 853 ·

Keep a (sealed) bag of frozen peas
in the freezer. It makes a perfect
icepack for bumps and sprains.

❋ *Give yourself a break:*
Healing—of any kind—takes time.
Take the time.

· 855 ·
Laughter is great medicine, so if you're
under the weather or feeling blue,
head straight for the comedy section
of your video rental store.

· 856 ·
Doodle as much as you want.

· 857 ·
Make quesadillas.

· 858 ·
Hang your clothes to dry
in the sun and breeze.

· 859 ·

Show pictures of your baby
to everyone you meet.

· 860 ·

Eat the cookie dough before it's baked.

· 861 ·

Visit Washington, D.C., at
cherry blossom time.

· 862 ·

Cancel your plans and stay in
on a wildly rainy day.

· 863 ·

Have your hair colored to hide the gray.

· 864 ·

Dress against your type and
surprise everyone.

❋ *Give yourself a break:*
When you can't crack a problem,
get help. Ask your smartest friend
to brainstorm with you.

· 866 ·
Don't waste time on regrets.

· 867 ·
Don't waste energy on battles you
don't really care about winning.

· 868 ·
Dress up and go to a piano bar.
Request your favorite song.

· 869 ·
Take a baking class and
learn to make bread or puff paste
or perfect cakes.

· 870 ·

Indulge in a bottle of top-quality,
extra virgin olive oil.

· 871 ·

Buy one of those Plexiglas stands that holds
your cookbook open to the right page.

· 872 ·

Make yourself a huge chef's salad for dinner.

· 873 ·

Invite your cat to sit on your lap
while you work at your computer.

· 874 ·

Have extra electrical outlets installed.

· 875 ·

Get a coffee machine that starts
automatically, so the coffee will
be ready when you stagger into
the kitchen in the morning.

· 876 ·

Get yourself an electric cup warmer
that keeps your tea or coffee hot
for as long as it takes to drink it.

· 877 ·

Watch travel videos and
pretend you're taking a trip.

· 878 ·

Program your automatic
dialer with the numbers of
your best buddies.

· 879 ·

Enjoy the intimacy of
your close friendships.

· 880 ·

Walk away from grumpy, snide, mean, unpleasant, sarcastic, condescending, nasty, hostile, malicious people.

· 881 ·

Make a list of the twenty-five best things that have ever happened to you.

· 882 ·

Write down your dreams when you wake up in the morning.

· 883 ·

Visit giant-size Lucy the Margate Elephant, now a children's library in Margate, New Jersey.

❀ *Give yourself a break:*
Admit that you *can* do that certain something you've always wanted to do. You know what it is. Now get to it!

· 885 ·

Water your garden at sunrise.
Watch the colors change from refreshingly
cool to glowingly warm as
the light increases.

· 886 ·

Take home a
snow globe and
shake it up often.

· 887 ·

Toss out those jelly glasses and treat
yourself to an attractive set of matching
glasses in three basic sizes.

· 888 ·

Try a Bellini: one part peach puree
or peach nectar stirred lightly
into three parts dry sparkling
wine or champagne.

· 889 ·

Buy yourself a beautiful evening bag.

· 890 ·

Take a date to a black-tie charity event.

· 891 ·

Wear lacy, brief, pretty silk
underwear for romance.

· 892 ·

Wear long-sleeved, long-legged silk
underwear for warmth.

· 893 ·

Smooth your heels and elbows
with a pumice stone.

· 894 ·

Brush your hair until it shines.

· 895 ·

Take a trip to the desert at sunrise
or sunset to see the stark beauty.

· 896 ·

Before bed, rub hands and feet with
lots of moisturizer. Put on thin cotton
gloves and socks and let the moisturizer
do its magic while you sleep.

· 897 ·

Keep a tube of lip balm in a pocket
of your winter jacket and winter coat,
for soothing chapped lips on the fly.

· 898 ·

Buy shoes with Velcro closings,
especially if you have stiff finger joints.

· 899 ·

If your glasses pinch your nose or feel too
tight over your ears, get new frames.

· 900 ·

Have your windshield cleaned.

· 901 ·

Insist on your privacy.

· 902 ·

Stop reading magazines that
tell you how to live, imply you're
falling short of the mark, and give you
a million more chores to do to meet
the standards *they* set for you.

· 903 ·

Start strength training with weights,
to feel strong and powerful.

· 904 ·

Have a wildly good time at
Mardi Gras in New Orleans.

· 905 ·

Be sure the household chores
are divided fairly.

· 906 ·

Suck on a lollipop.

· 907 ·

Eat buttered graham crackers with jelly.

· 908 ·

Order the fried chicken instead
of the grilled chicken.

· 909 ·

Have a nutritionist design the
perfect diet for you.

· 910 ·

Stroll, instead of charging
along at top speed.

· 911 ·

Switch from a messy old address
book to a spiffy new Rolodex.

· 912 ·

Heat the dinner plates.

· 913 ·

Build a tree house in your backyard.

❀ *Give yourself a break:*
Forgive yourself for whatever terrible
mistakes you think you've made.
Get on with your life.

· 915 ·

Play duets with a friend.

· 916 ·

Play music with a group of friends—jazz,
country, rock and roll, chamber music.

· 917 ·

Make thick slices of French toast.

· 918 ·

Get a vanity license plate.

· 919 ·

Order movie tickets by phone to avoid
the long lines on Saturday night.

· 920 ·

Plant your front "lawn" with
pachysandra instead of grass,
so you won't have to mow it.

· 921 ·

Stock the freezer with a couple of
delicious vegetable pies or quiches for
nights when you can't bear to cook.

· 922 ·

Have your hair done at home.

· 923 ·

Be sure to use a wrist rest when
working at your computer.

· 924 ·

Head straight from the office
to the gym, have a great workout,
and go home feeling energized.

· 925 ·

Convert one of your countertops
to butcher block.

· 926 ·

Behave in a way that will get you
what you want. Or, to put it differently,
stop behaving in a way that prevents you
from getting what you want.

· 927 ·

Have a professional help you compile
and design your résumé.

· 928 ·

Start that small business you've been
dreaming about for years.

· 929 ·

Have a classy letterhead
printed for yourself.

· 930 ·

Express your opinions—to the
hometown newspaper, to your local
politicians, to your national politicians.

· 931 ·

Hire a genealogist to find out all
about your family tree.

· 932 ·

Visit the immigration museum at
Ellis Island in New York City.

· 933 ·

Take yourself out on a date:
Dress nicely and do exactly what
you want. Go to a movie or show.
Eat where you want to eat. Go home
when you want to go home.

· 934 ·

Make love in the magical hours of early
morning, when the day is not yet quite real.

· 935 ·

Make love very late at night, when there's
no one in the world but the two of you.

· 936 ·

In summer, go up to the roof of your
apartment building and stargaze.

· 937 ·

If streetlights keep you up at
night and dawn wakes you too early,
get blackout shades.

· 938 ·

Squinting makes wrinkles.
Wear sunglasses and stop squinting.

· 939 ·

Sleep in a comfy, oversized T-shirt.

· 940 ·

Work up a good sweat at the gym,
then take a l-o-n-g shower.

· 941 ·

Buy really good pasta instead of
the supermarket brand.

· 942 ·

Eat peanut brittle.

· 943 ·

Get a padded bicycle seat.

· 944 ·

Set a goal and head toward it.

· 945 ·

Keep a few little wrapped candies in your
coat pocket for treats along the way.

· 946 ·

Lighten your load: Sort through your
makeup collection and get rid of what
you don't use anymore.

❀ *Give yourself a break:*
If you're overbooked this week,
reschedule some dates to a week
when you have more time.

· 948 ·

When you're angry, tear paper (grocery bags, newspapers, catalogs, junk mail) and throw it around the room *with abandon*.

· 949 ·

Laugh at your mistakes.

· 950 ·

Teach your kids how to prepare one decent dinner, and call on them to make it when you need pampering.

· 951 ·

Teach your kids how to do their own laundry.

· 952 ·

Lighten, brighten, and organize the laundry room—then you (and everyone else) won't hate being there.

· 953 ·

Install a phone in the laundry room,
so you can chat and fold at the same time.

· 954 ·

Keep a file of household and office
services, so you know whom to call
when you've got a problem.

· 955 ·

Go out for brunch and have something
you never make at home: eggs Benedict,
Belgian waffles, blueberry pancakes.

· 956 ·

Call a friend and trade apartments
or houses for a weekend or
week-long change of scene.

· 957 ·

Read memoirs and journals for juicy
glimpses into other lives.

❀ *Do yourself a favor:*
Stop fighting the facts of who you are.
Stop beating yourself up for
not being someone else.

· 959 ·

Put a bouquet of
miniature roses
on your desk.

· 960 ·

Take two: For two minutes, just breathe,
stretch, and take a break.

· 961 ·

Even if you don't ski, go to a ski lodge,
sit by the fire, and drink hot
chocolate or hot toddies.

· 962 ·

Go out for the day,
and leave your calendar and
address book at home.

· 963 ·

Take the escalator instead
of the stairs. Take the elevator
instead of the escalator.

· 964 ·

Eat all the snacks in the little bowl
when you're having a drink at a bar.

· 965 ·

Cook artichokes and eat
only the hearts.

· 966 ·

Fly the Concorde to Paris.

· 967 ·

Hire someone to come in and
groom your pet, or take your pet
regularly to a grooming salon.

✳ *Join a country club.*

✳ *Don't join a country club.*

· 970 ·

Swim in a secluded
mountain pool.

❋ *Give yourself a break:*
Enjoy *this* day and don't think beyond it.
Let tomorrow take care of itself.

· 972 ·

Eat whipped cream.

· 973 ·

Break off pieces of a chocolate bar,
dunk them in peanut butter, and eat.

· 974 ·

Go to a baseball game
and do the whole enchilada—
baseball cap, team sweatshirt,
hot dogs, Cracker Jacks,
ice cream.

· 975 ·

Get yourself a bulletin board,
so you can tack up pictures of
your family and friends, reminders,
jokes, poems—a changing
album of your daily life.

· 976 ·

Show off your collectibles in
a handsome display case.

· 977 ·

If you love to cook, treat
yourself to an exotic and wonderful
ingredient: a tiny tube of real saffron,
an ounce of dried porcini mushrooms,
glacé chestnuts, candied ginger.

· 978 ·

Give away all those appliances
and gadgets you almost never use:
hot trays, pasta makers, waffle irons,
orange squeezers, apple peelers.

· 979 ·

Install under-the-cabinet
lighting in your kitchen.

· 980 ·

Grow a pot of chives on your kitchen
windowsill. Snip and use often.

· 981 ·

Make yourself a May basket—
a bouquet of spring flowers tied
with a rainbow of satin ribbons.

· 982 ·

After every major chore
(such as spring cleaning)
be sure to give yourself a treat.

❀ *Give yourself a break:*
Don't let your kids' planned activities
run your life. Set limits. You need time
for *your* activities too.

· 984 ·

Read a rich, rewarding series of novels in
which you really get to know the characters:
The Forsyte Saga by John Galsworthy,
Trollope's *Palliser* books, the
Anne of Green Gables stories.

· 985 ·

Designate a special place for your
specs and learn to put them there,
so you *stop losing your glasses*.

· 986 ·

Use lovely notecards for your
thank-yous. Your friends will
appreciate you even more.

· 987 ·

Enjoy a leisurely browse in
a hardware store, pet shop, kitchen
emporium, gourmet market.

· 988 ·

See the rocky coast of Maine.

· 989 ·

Tune in to the different kinds
of music at the listening stations
at a big tape-and-CD store.

· 990 ·

When you can't sleep, make yourself a
cup of hot milk with a spoonful each of
honey and brandy. Sit by a window and
watch the night sky until you're drowsy.

· 991 ·

Make a quilt for your baby.

· 992 ·

Read your high school diary.

· 993 ·

Send a check to an organization that's doing
something in which you believe deeply.

· 994 ·

Eat as many nachos as you want.

· 995 ·

Clown around: Jump on a pogo stick.
Walk on stilts. Pedal a unicycle.

· 996 ·
Get a good salad spinner.

· 997 ·
Have your drapes cleaned
professionally.

· 998 ·
Buy two pairs of any pants
or jeans that fit you perfectly
and look terrific.

· 999 ·
Cut your hair short.

· 1000 ·
Let your hair grow.

· 1001 ·
Have a black-and-white soda
and a black-and-white cookie.

· 1002 ·

Carve a jack-o'-lantern
for your front porch.

· 1003 ·

Find out who makes the best
box lunches in your town, then buy
two and whisk your honeybun
off to a surprise picnic.

· 1004 ·

Buy the sleeping bag of your dreams.

· 1005 ·

Wear cheerful red rubber boots to
keep your feet dry in the rain.

· 1006 ·

Keep a tube of anti-itch goop
by your bed for middle-of-the-night
mosquito bites.

· 1007 ·

Have someone put up the storm windows
before it gets seriously cold.

· 1008 ·

Have someone bring in a large load of
firewood and stack it by the fireplace,
ready and waiting.

· 1009 ·

Have someone put up the window screens
before the mosquitoes invade.

· 1010 ·

Get yourself a stunning hat to
keep off the July sun.

· 1011 ·

Celebrate August with peaches:
peach jam, peach cobbler, peach pie,
peach chutney, peach shortcake.

· 1012 ·

Flag down the ice-cream man and
have one of your all-time favorites.

· 1013 ·

Learn how to use the computer
cataloging system at the library,
so you can find any book you want.

· 1014 ·

Always check your coat in restaurants.

· 1015 ·

Give yourself more room:
Build shelves into a closet you
don't really need for clothes.

· 1016 ·

Don't try to go it alone: Join Weight
Watchers, attend AA or Al-Anon meetings,
go to church, talk to your friends.

· 1017 ·

Keep in touch: Get a beeper.

· 1018 ·

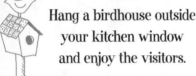

Hang a birdhouse outside
your kitchen window
and enjoy the visitors.

· 1019 ·

Snuggle with your pussycat.

· 1020 ·

Buy yourself a soft, warm shawl.

· 1021 ·

Make garlic bread for dinner.

✿ *Give yourself a break:*
If you have an emotionally difficult task to
do (such as planning a funeral, or visiting a
nursing home or hospital), ask your brother
or sister or friend to accompany you.

· 1023 ·

Plan a January or February
vacation in a sunny, warm place.

· 1024 ·

Do something creative that
gives you satisfaction: draw, write,
make music, embroider, cook, take
photographs, invent computer games,
make toys, build a playhouse.

· 1025 ·

Drive a fire engine in the next
hometown parade.

· 1026 ·

Go to an auction and bid on
your favorite item.

· 1027 ·

Decide when the time is right to ask
for a raise, and ask for it.

· 1028 ·

Buy the soundtrack to a show
or movie you loved.

· 1029 ·

Treat yourself to a countertop rotisserie.

· 1030 ·

Ask your partner to
massage your neck.

· 1031 ·

Eat something you haven't eaten
since you were a child: a chocolate malt,
candy apple, animal crackers,
Mallomars, alphabet soup.

· 1032 ·

Reread your favorite Dr. Seuss books.

· 1033 ·

Go into therapy.

· 1034 ·

Shine your shoes and boots.

· 1035 ·

Take an early morning, barefoot
walk on grass that's still dewy.

· 1036 ·

Start an add-a-pearl necklace. Reward
yourself with another pearl for each
birthday, promotion, or life-changing event.

· 1037 ·

Take a trip around your house or
apartment collecting every item you
don't like. Give them away.

❋ *Give yourself a break:*
Let go of the past. Stop trying
to do *everything* you were able
to do ten years ago.

· 1039 ·

Hire somebody to clean the venetian blinds.

· 1040 ·

Get a new shower curtain liner. Get a new shower curtain, too, while you're at it.

· 1041 ·

Toss out that creepy old bathroom rug and pick up one that's soft and thick and colorful.

· 1042 ·

Put a magazine rack in the bathroom.

· 1043 ·

Read James Thurber's hilarious story, "The Night the Bed Fell."

· 1044 ·

Watch home movies.

· 1045 ·

Invite your grandchildren (or your nieces
and nephews) to visit for a few days.
Indulge them shamelessly.

· 1046 ·

Start an aquarium of
incredibly beautiful fish.

· 1047 ·

Eat as many soft-shell crabs as you want.

· 1048 ·

Work out for half an hour, four
mornings a week.

· 1049 ·

Buy a sexy black dress.

· 1050 ·
Put pretty ornaments, barrettes,
or combs in your hair.

· 1051 ·
Leave for your vacation
on your birthday.

· 1052 ·
Order custom-made fortune cookies,
with terrific fortunes written by you.
Predict only rosy futures.

· 1053 ·
State your needs and don't back down.

· 1054 ·
Give yourself permission to feel bad.

· 1055 ·
Give yourself permission to feel good.

· 1056 ·
Give yourself permission to fail.

· 1057 ·
Give yourself permission to succeed.

· 1058 ·
Give yourself permission to change.

· 1059 ·
Give yourself permission to
be who you are.

· 1060 ·
Allow yourself to fantasize about
anything. No one but you will know your
thoughts, and you don't have to do a thing
about them if you don't want to.

· 1061 ·
Consult a career counselor.

· 1062 ·

Buy yourself a great piece
of costume jewelry.

· 1063 ·

Learn to water-ski.

❀ *Do yourself a favor:*
Stop worrying about the weird outfits
your children want to wear.

· 1065 ·

Read only the newspaper's fun stuff: the
gossip column, the horoscope, the comics.

· 1066 ·

Feel free to have lots of opened jars
of jam and jelly in the fridge.

· 1067 ·

Claim a separate closet for your clothes.

· 1068 ·

Make paper snowflakes and tape
them to your windows.

❋ *Give yourself a break:*
Declare a one-day moratorium
on boring chores.

· 1070 ·

Host an ice cream party,
with three flavors and lots of toppings:
chocolate and butterscotch sauces, sliced
bananas, chopped nuts, toasted coconut,
crumbled brownies, multicolored
sprinkles, miniature chocolate chips.

· 1071 ·

Let someone give *you* a party.

· 1072 ·

Get tickets to your favorite local TV show.

· 1073 ·
Stay inside, cozy and warm,
while a blizzard rages outside.

· 1074 ·
Let your partner take good care of you
when you're down with the flu.

· 1075 ·
Take life easy with a bed desk
(a special tray with storage compartments
and tilt-up top), so you can work
comfortably in bed.

· 1076 ·
Sit on your lover's lap and let
him rock you like a baby.

· 1077 ·
Eat soft-boiled eggs topped
with bits of buttered toast.

· 1078 ·

Have your morning coffee on the
porch, early, in spring or summer.

· 1079 ·

Put on your rubber boots and
grab your umbrella for a solo walk
in the rain. Lose yourself in the sounds
and smells. Ponder life.

· 1080 ·

Rethink your perfume.
Change it to suit who you are *now.*

· 1081 ·

Replace the ugly buttons on a
nice piece of clothing.

· 1082 ·

Buy yourself a fancy
beaded sweater.

· 1083 ·

Be naughty.

· 1084 ·

Be shocking.

· 1085 ·

Be wicked.

❋ *Go to Disneyland.*

❋ *Don't go to Disneyland.*

· 1088 ·

Fall asleep holding hands with your partner.

· 1089 ·

Get a new mattress.

· 1090 ·

Stop living out of crates and boxes,
and turn that house into a home.

· 1091 ·

Expose the handsome old brick wall hiding
under all that plaster and paint.

· 1092 ·

Have your floors sanded and stained.

· 1093 ·

Lock yourself in the bathroom and have a
do-it-yourself, head-to-toe beauty treatment:
shampoo and conditioning, body
moisturizing, foot-softening, lots more.

❀ *Do yourself a favor:*

First impressions are important, but bad
ones *aren't* fatal. Don't waste time crying;
get out there and do damage control.

· 1095 ·

Keep a sewing repair box handy,
and nip trouble in the bud when a
button pops off or a hem rips.

· 1096 ·

Invest in a few basic tools
(screwdriver, pliers, small saw,
hammer, nails), so you have
them when you need them.

· 1097 ·

If it ain't broke, don't fix it.

· 1098 ·

If it *is* broken, either fix it,
get it fixed, or throw it out.

· 1099 ·

Eliminate the busywork in your
life to find more time for fun.

❀ *Give yourself a break:*
Leave the dishes
until tomorrow.

· 1101 ·
Hit that terrific flea market
at the end of the day when the
prices drop w-a-y d-o-w-n.

· 1102 ·
Throw an elegant party, so you
can wear your fanciest dress.

· 1103 ·
Record the song you've written.

· 1104 ·
Try a sauna.

· 1105 ·
Spend a little money on yourself.

· 1106 ·
Spend a lot of money on yourself.

· 1107 ·

Phone-chat with your best friend
six times a day.

· 1108 ·

Secretly check out all the new
Barbie dolls and their outfits.

· 1109 ·

Drop in on your old elementary
school and feel like a grown-up.

· 1110 ·

Go on a Great Cookie Hunt: Visit every
bakery in town. Taste-test at least two
cookies in each one. Pick your favorites.

· 1111 ·

Play Frisbee.

· 1112 ·

Keep nice, new, untorn road maps
in your glove compartment.

· 1113 ·

When you're on a long driving trip,
stop at every little roadside attraction
and buy silly souvenirs.

· 1114 ·

Hire a local craftsperson to decorate
your walls or floors with sponging,
spattering, or stenciling.

· 1115 ·

Wear flannel-lined jeans so
you'll be utterly warm.

· 1116 ·

Find *the* T-shirt that looks great on you,
and buy five of them.

❀ *Give yourself a break:*
Don't volunteer to have Thanksgiving
at *your* house this year.

· 1118 ·

Have a video-fest of classic sci-fi films:
*The Fly, Invasion of the Body Snatchers,
The Day the Earth Stood Still, The
Incredible Shrinking Man, When Worlds
Collide, The Invisible Man.*

· 1119 ·

Put a night-light in the bathroom.

· 1120 ·

Do what it takes to stop yourself from
worrying: Double-check that you turned off
the oven or the iron or the computer, locked
the front door, closed the windows, turned
on the answering machine, and so on.

· 1121 ·

Keep a few cans of comforting chicken
noodle soup in the pantry for days when
you're stuck in bed with a cold.

· 1122 ·

Treat yourself to a pot big enough to boil
the right amount of water for pasta.

· 1123 ·

Learn to make sensational
marinara sauce.

· 1124 ·

Buy really good bread instead of the fluffy
kind. Try a crusty Italian round, French
baguette, sourdough, or seven-grain loaf.

· 1125 ·

Go to a French bakery and have
pain au chocolat—brioche swirled
with bittersweet chocolate.

· 1126 ·

Sip a warm golden cognac
in front of the fire.

· 1127 ·

Graduate from instant coffee
to real brewed coffee.

· 1128 ·

Graduate from tea bags to
real brewed tea.

· 1129 ·

Snuggle in bed, spoon-style.

· 1130 ·

Make buttercream frosting
and put it on anything.

· 1131 ·

Wear sheer, silky pantyhose to work.

· 1132 ·

Never go out without something to read
tucked in your pocket or handbag.

· 1133 ·

Get a good-looking carrying case for
your laptop or notebook computer.

· 1134 ·

Increase your storage capacity by putting
an artist's taboret (a rolling cart with
shelves and drawers) near your desk.

· 1135 ·

Buy a small space heater
and put it under your desk to keep
your feet and legs toasty.

❀ *Do yourself a favor:*

Keep your driveway clear of bicycles, toys,
gardening tools, and other hazards.

· 1137 ·

Ask your partner to go out and warm up
the car for you on a winter morning.

· 1138 ·

Go berry-picking on a hot summer day when the air is so still that you can hear bees humming.

· 1139 ·

Lose your heart to an adorable new batch of kittens or puppies.

· 1140 ·

Wear a feather boa.

Have a baby.

Don't have a baby.

· 1143 ·

Hire a landscape designer to come up with a master plan.

· 1144 ·

In autumn, brighten your home
with branches of colorful leaves,
bittersweet, firethorn.

· 1145 ·

Go to the Homecoming Weekend game.

· 1146 ·

Stash away a picnic basket that includes
paper plates and napkins, plastic utensils
and glasses, tablecloth, salt and pepper.
Just add food and you're ready to go.

· 1147 ·

Go on a mountain hike. Take a book
and a lunch, find a flat rock next to
a waterfall, and spend the day.

· 1148 ·

Invest in a foot massage machine.

· 1149 ·

Wear cashmere-blend knee
socks under your slacks.

· 1150 ·

Take a Wednesday afternoon off for a mini-
vacation—a drive in the country, a stroll on
the beach, a trip to a museum. Top it off
with a great meal at a new restaurant.

· 1151 ·

Agree to do something you don't want
to do, then accidentally-on-purpose get
a headache at the last minute.

· 1152 ·

Play computer solitaire for hours on end.

· 1153 ·

Get the Sunday paper on Saturday night,
so you don't have to leave the
house on Sunday morning.

· 1154 ·

Put your loose change in a
jar every day. When the
jar is full, use the money
for a special treat.

· 1155 ·

Plan to do high-focus, stressful,
or tiring chores *only* at the time of day
when you have the most energy.

· 1156 ·

Decide not to feel guilty for your
perceived shortcomings.

· 1157 ·

Leave the heavy lifting
to someone else.

· 1158 ·

Impatient? Get a Polaroid camera.

· 1159 ·

Go to a full-service gas station
and let them do it all.

· 1160 ·

Create a small desk area in your kitchen,
with pad, pencils, portable phone,
phonebooks, Rolodex, calendar.

· 1161 ·

Tell the kids to set the table
for tomorrow's breakfast before
they go to bed.

· 1162 ·

Get up fifteen minutes earlier, so
your mornings are more relaxed.

· 1163 ·

Leave the house fifteen minutes earlier, so
you don't have to rush to school or work.

· 1164 ·

Vacuum the inside of your car.
It'll be a pleasure to drive.

· 1165 ·

Collect all your clothes that need
repair and take them to a local tailor.

 Give yourself a break:
Let someone else take a turn at
being the leader—of the scout troop,
the garden club, the church supper,
the book group, and so on.

· 1167 ·

Let your partner make dinner
for *you* for a change.

· 1168 ·

Learn how to work all the bells and whistles
on your new fax machine, answering
machine, camera, CD player, and other toys.

· 1169 ·

Ignore the alarm clock and
go back to sleep.

· 1170 ·

Take a cruise—to the Caribbean,
across the ocean, through the fjords
of Norway, down the Mississippi.

· 1171 ·

Head for your city's lake,
and rent a rowboat for a few
hours of idle paddling.

· 1172 ·

Deck yourself out in an authentic,
striped, French sailor's jersey.

· 1173 ·

Treat yourself to a
good-looking wine rack.

· 1174 ·

Buy a chubby slice of scrumptious liver,
duck, or pheasant pâté and eat it
with warm toast points.

· 1175 ·

Have a piñata at your birthday party.
Margaritas are good too.

· 1176 ·

Relive your memories: Read a book
(especially one with a lot of pictures) about
the decade you feel most attached to.

· 1177 ·

Cook yourself a truly delicious dinner and
toast yourself with a glass of excellent wine.

· 1178 ·

Become a regular at a favorite
restaurant, and you'll always get
a good table and fine service.

· 1179 ·

Take home all the fancy stationery
and postcards from the leather
folder in your hotel room.

· 1180 ·

Take home all the little soaps
and shampoos too.

· 1181 ·

Put a birdbath in your garden.

· 1182 ·

Change your bad old showerhead to a good
new one that dials smoothly from massage
to spray—and saves water as well.

· 1183 ·

Hire someone to shampoo your rugs.

· 1184 ·

Have your couch recovered.

· 1185 ·

Turn your mattress.

· 1186 ·

Have an overstuffed
sandwich.

· 1187 ·

Get a new cutting board.

· 1188 ·

Gorge on batter-fried onion rings.

· 1189 ·

Lie back in bed with at least four pillows.
Watch the soaps.

❁ *Give yourself a break:*
Keep your plans simple.
Think no-frills. Do things the
easier way. Streamline.

· 1191 ·
Do whatever helps but doesn't harm:
support groups, family therapy,
communication training, parenting
workshops, personal growth seminars.

· 1192 ·
Slink around in leather—
jacket, dress, or slacks.

· 1193 ·
Wear rings on every finger.

✳ *Shave your legs.*

✳ *Don't shave your legs.*

· 1196 ·
Call him just to hear his voice.

· 1197 ·
Call your best friend for no reason at all.

· 1198 ·

Wear your wedding dress to
your anniversary party.

· 1199 ·

If you can't afford French
champagne, pamper yourself with one
of the great American sparklers.

· 1200 ·

Watch the fabulous old Fred and
Ginger films: *Top Hat*, *Swing Time*,
and *Shall We Dance?*

· 1201 ·

Go for it: A classy felt fedora will make
you look like the sport you are.

· 1202 ·

Stand up straight. You'll look better,
and it's a lot easier to breathe that way.

· 1203 ·

Get your wardrobe into shape:
Sew on buttons. Mend holes. Stitch
up that torn hem or ripped seam.

· 1204 ·

Can't afford a top-of-the-line hair stylist?
Sign up for a cut or coloring on training
night, when carefully supervised
assistants test their skills.

�֍ *Do yourself a favor:*

Declare a one-day, worry-free holiday.

· 1206 ·

Have a cappuccino with whipped cream,
chocolate shavings, and cinnamon.

· 1207 ·

Throw out your stale spices and
herbs and buy new ones.

· 1208 ·

Gobble up videos of food films: *Babette's Feast; Big Night; Like Water for Chocolate; Tampopo; Eat, Drink, Man, Woman.*

· 1209 ·

If a friend wants to pick up the lunch tab, don't make a fuss. Thank her graciously— and enjoy being pampered.

· 1210 ·

Treat yourself to a jar of authentic mango chutney.

· 1211 ·

Make a big pot of rice and all the wonderful little condiments that go with curry—and don't bother making the curry.

· 1212 ·

Pamper yourself with heat: a steamy bath
at the end of the day, the hot licks of a
rock band, the hottest new style, hot cereal
for breakfast, hot-to-trot friends.

· 1213 ·

Pamper yourself with cold: a splash of
ocean surf, the chill of an October night, iced
bubbly, cool jazz, frozen fruit Popsicles.

· 1214 ·

Give yourself a pair of warm,
fuzzy bedroom slippers.

❀ *Do yourself a favor:*
Act on your intuition.
Follow your hunches.

· 1216 ·

Get carried away at a great parade—ethnic,
historical, holiday, sports, ticker tape.

· 1217 ·

Go to a karaoke bar, grab the
mike, and perform!

· 1218 ·

Wear anything you want to,
whether it's in good taste or not.

· 1219 ·

Improve the flavor of your next batch
of cookies: Use high-quality, pure
vanilla extract from Madagascar.

· 1220 ·

Visit an American island: Key West,
Sanibel, Block Island, Nantucket,
Santa Catalina, Maui, Deer Isle, Edisto,
Padre Island, Manhattan.

· 1221 ·

Go bird-watching.

· 1222 ·

Track down your old lover and
satisfy your curiosity.

· 1223 ·

Swing on the monkey bars.

· 1224 ·

Play miniature golf.

· 1225 ·

Order from room service.

· 1226 ·

Have a little toast with your butter.

· 1227 ·

Request a calling card from your long
distance phone company.

· 1228 ·

Get an up-to-the-minute fax machine.

· 1229 ·

Vote early so you'll feel virtuous all day.

· 1230 ·

Send in your contribution but don't go
to that charity event you loathe.

· 1231 ·

Call a talk show and calmly state your
carefully reasoned opinion.

· 1232 ·

Walk through a forest very softly.
Watch. Listen.

 Give yourself a break:
When you have a tough decision to make,
write a list of the pros and cons.
Base your thinking on your list.

· 1234 ·

Tell your family members kindly but firmly
that you don't want their advice today.

· 1235 ·

Tell your partner lovingly but firmly that
you don't want his or her advice today.

· 1236 ·

Acknowledge how well you're really
doing. Be proud of yourself.

· 1237 ·

Do a dress rehearsal before attending
a glam party. Try on *everything*,
including jewelry, and do a full makeup too.
Practice makes perfect.

· 1238 ·

Have an Academy Awards festival:
Rent the videos of the Oscar-winning
films of the past three years.

· 1239 ·

Have a strawberry festival: strawberry
shortcake, strawberry ice cream,
strawberry cheesecake, strawberry tarts.

· 1240 ·

Display your most treasured
plates and platters.

· 1241 ·

If you've always wanted a
reclining chair, get one.

· 1242 ·

At the first hint of spring, arrange
branches of forsythia and pussywillow
in a big vase in a warm room.

· 1243 ·

Make an Easter basket filled
with marshmallow chicks, jelly
beans, and chocolate bunnies.

· 1244 ·

Hire a gardener to get your
flower beds into shape.

· 1245 ·

Eat as much new asparagus as
you've ever wanted—hot with butter
or cold with vinaigrette.

· 1246 ·

Do a few stretches the moment
you get out of bed.

· 1247 ·

Put your wallet and glasses in
your pocket, and spend a day *without*
the burden of your handbag.

· 1248 ·

Oh, go ahead—call your old high
school sweetheart for a date.

Do yourself a favor:
Try not to overeat. If you overeat,
you'll feel bloated and uncomfortable,
so be good to yourself and don't do it.

· 1250 ·
Take as long as you need to recover
from a terrible loss. There are no
shortcuts through grief.

· 1251 ·
Get yourself a thick terry-cloth robe
for warmth and comfort.

· 1252 ·
Sleep on a featherbed.

· 1253 ·
Ask your partner to pick
you up after work.

· 1254 ·

Ask a good friend to check
up on you by phone a couple of
times during a bad day.

· 1255 ·

Read some great children's books: the
Little House series, *Alice in Wonderland*,
Chronicles of Narnia by C. S. Lewis, Roald
Dahl's books, *A Wrinkle in Time* by
Madeleine L'Engle, E. B. White's *Stuart Little*
and *The Trumpet of the Swan*.

· 1256 ·

Have someone meet you at the plane.

· 1257 ·

Go home early.

· 1258 ·

Eat a hot, buttered fresh roll.

· 1259 ·

Eat warm gingerbread cake
with cool whipped cream.

· 1260 ·

Join a choir and belt out those
songs or hymns.

· 1261 ·

Go for the gold—gold pen,
gold bracelet, gold cuff links,
gold watch, gold earrings.

✳ *Run the marathon.*

✳ *Don't run the marathon.*

· 1264 ·

If you don't have time for professional
massages, consider a flexible, deep heat
body massager you can use at home.

· 1265 ·

Have enough socks for at least
two weeks. Ditto underwear.

· 1266 ·

Invite friends over for a
spur-of-the-moment, on-the-fly,
easy-to-make pasta dinner.

· 1267 ·

Learn to drive a stick shift.

· 1268 ·

Live in T-shirts
and overalls.

· 1269 ·

Build a brick barbecue in the backyard.

· 1270 ·

Grill your a) steak, b) shrimp, c) chicken,
or d) vegetables to perfection.

· 1271 ·

Treat yourself to a well-made
pepper mill and a supply of
whole peppercorns.

· 1272 ·

Make a trade: Exchange your homegrown
lettuce and tomatoes for help with your
tennis game, your skill at car repair for a
week of homemade frozen dinners, your
bookkeeping talent for music lessons.

· 1273 ·

Prepare salad dressing from
scratch instead of using those
packets of powder.

· 1274 ·

Build a pass-through from kitchen
to dining area. Then you won't have
to run around so much.

· 1275 ·

Ask for more: more cheese on your pizza,
more sprinkles on your ice cream cone,
more sauerkraut on your hot dog.

· 1276 ·

Ask for less: less nagging, less
argument, less criticism.

· 1277 ·

Rearrange the furniture the
way *you* want it.

· 1278 ·

Put a small rug next to your side
of the bed, so you don't have to put
your bare feet on the cold floor.

· 1279 ·

Refuse to throw away that
old flannel blazer you love.

· 1280 ·

Buy a big slab of heavenly Valrhona
or Callebaut chocolate.

· 1281 ·

If you're a pack rat, permission is
hereby granted to keep everything.
But try to organize your stuff neatly,
so you can get to it when you want it.

· 1282 ·

Rent videos *you* like. Don't worry
about what your spouse, your kids,
or your roommate wants to see.

❀ *Give yourself a break:*
Don't even *think* of ironing
the sheets, the T-shirts, the
pillowcases, the pajamas.

· 1284 ·

Let the bag-packer put your grocery bags
in the cart, wheel the cart to your car,
and transfer the bags to the trunk.

· 1285 ·

Ask the phone company for two (or more)
sets of phone books—one set for each
phone, so you don't have to run downstairs
every time you need to look up a number.

· 1286 ·

Treat yourself
to the one piece
of pastry you crave but never,
ever allow yourself.

· 1287 ·

Short of putting a lampshade
on your head, live it up
and enjoy the party.

· 1288 ·
File your taxes early to get
your refund sooner.

· 1289 ·
Leave the mistletoe up all year—
and take advantage of it.

· 1290 ·
Read a good-news-only newspaper.

· 1291 ·
Go back to sleep for twenty minutes.

· 1292 ·
Buy a pair of fabulous
suede gloves.

· 1293 ·
Test-drive a Ferrari. Or a Jaguar.
Or a Corvette.

· 1294 ·

Keep an emergency chocolate
bar in the freezer.

· 1295 ·

Punch your pillow until you feel better.

· 1296 ·

Scream until you feel better.

· 1297 ·

Check into a hotel for a night,
to escape from everything and everyone.
Get a good night's sleep.

· 1298 ·

Have a good cry.

· 1299 ·

Make a list of the satisfying
things in your life.

· 1300 ·
Smell the honeysuckle on a warm night.

· 1301 ·
Ask someone to teach you something
you want to learn: how to make bread,
how to use a computer, how to write
a résumé, how to put on mascara.

· 1302 ·
Listen to your favorite music on your
walk-around tape player.

· 1303 ·
Buy a large meringue. Slice off the top.
Fill with ice cream. Garnish with
fresh raspberries. Replace the top.
Eat immediately.

· 1304 ·
Grind your own coffee beans,
for sensational coffee.

· 1305 ·
Toss out those
crummy old dish
towels and pot holders,
and buy new ones.

· 1306 ·
Abolish the linen closet entirely:
Keep towels in the bathroom.
Keep sheets, pillowcases, and blankets
in the bedrooms they belong to.

· 1307 ·
Clear out the clutter in your home
workshop to give yourself room
for starting a new project.

· 1308 ·
Tell your significant other you need time
for yourself, and send him away for a couple
of days. Do *not* talk to him on the phone
while he's gone. Reunion will be sweet.

＊ *Put things back where they belong after you use them.*

 ＊ *Don't bother putting anything back until you have to.*

· 1311 ·

Hire a housekeeper to clean your house or apartment once a week or even once every two weeks.

· 1312 ·

Hire a baby-sitter and go off on your own for an afternoon. Do what you love most or miss most—shopping, a movie, a museum, a hike.

· 1313 ·

Visit a crafts fair to pick up handmade artwork—and absorb inspiration too.

· 1314 ·

Discover and explore the simplicity
and beauty of Shaker furniture.

· 1315 ·

Next time you're in a big city,
get a multicultural life: Visit the ethnic
neighborhoods. Try the food, shop
in the stores, chat with the people.

· 1316 ·

Spend a summer evening at a
concert or theatrical performance
in the park. Pack a delicious picnic
and a chilled bottle of wine.

· 1317 ·

Take a leisurely stroll through
a botanical garden.

· 1318 ·

Try an exotic fruit: mango, papaya,
casaba or Persian melon, starfruit,
Asian pear, pomegranate.

· 1319 ·

Subscribe to a travel magazine
or newsletter.

· 1320 ·

Change into a long, soft jersey pullover
dress when you get home from work.

· 1321 ·

When everyone else races out to ski or
skate or snowboard, stay home by the fire.

· 1322 ·

Read Shakespeare's sonnets.

· 1323 ·

Wear an orchid.

· 1324 ·
Have an entourage.

· 1325 ·
Hire someone to do your errands.

· 1326 ·
Sit down to afternoon tea at a luxe hotel
or restaurant— with tiny sandwiches,
miniature pastries, baby scones,
lots of butter and jam.

· 1327 ·
Drive a speedboat.

· 1328 ·
Start an investment club.

· 1329 ·
Take a child to the pond to feed
the ducks and geese.

· 1330 ·
Buy perfume instead of cologne.

· 1331 ·
Install wall-to-wall carpeting.

· 1332 ·
Collect scarves.

· 1333 ·
Shop a vintage clothing
store for a gorgeous bias-cut,
peach satin nightgown.
Wear it often.

· 1334 ·
Make a soufflé and eat it the
moment it comes out
of the oven.

· 1335 ·

Sit on a porch, deck, balcony,
or park bench and enjoy *l'heure bleu*—
that magical time between dusk
and dark, when the indigo sky is
flecked with just a few bright stars.

❋ *Give yourself a break:*
Expect a little less than perfection.

· 1337 ·

Fix a fancy Sunday brunch
and wash it down with mimosas—
champagne and orange
juice served icy cold.

· 1338 ·

Enjoy looking at sexy people
on the street.

· 1339 ·

Collect a variety of friends—shopping
friends, phone friends, heart-to-heart
friends, lunch friends.

· 1340 ·

Hire live musicians for your next
big party: a pianist, a string quartet,
a guitarist, a jazz ensemble.

✳ *Go camping in one of our
wonderful national parks.*

✳ *Refuse to go camping
anywhere at all.*

· 1343 ·

Give a fund-raising party for a candidate
about whom you feel passionate.

· 1344 ·

Support a charity you believe in.

· 1345 ·

Get a checking account of your own.

· 1346 ·

Save a dollar a day.

· 1347 ·

Pay off and retire one credit card.

 Do yourself a favor:
Firmly steer around negative
people who discourage you from doing
what you think is right for you.

· 1349 ·

Start a family tradition that *you* love.

· 1350 ·

Put a few beautiful objects
on your mantelpiece, so you can
enjoy them daily.

· 1351 ·

Use the right tools for the job.

· 1352 ·

Invest in a small, handheld,
recharging vacuum cleaner, so you don't
have to haul out the big machine.

· 1353 ·

Get a good backpack and carry
your stuff on your back instead of
in your arms or in shopping bags.
It will leave your hands free too.

· 1354 ·

Buy an extra pair of sunglasses against
the inevitable day when you lose your
usual pair at the beach or the lake.

· 1355 ·

Ride your bicycle to work.

· 1356 ·

Spend a whole day at a state or county
fair. Do it all: pet the goats, admire the
prizewinning cakes, eat silly food,
ride the Ferris wheel at sundown.

· 1357 ·

Enjoy an autumn game from the
bleachers, armed with a thick blanket
and a thermos of hot cider.

· 1358 ·

Go Brit for a night: Have a sherry
party with Stilton cheese, water biscuits,
and walnuts in the shell.

· 1359 ·

Make real applesauce,
spiked with applejack.

· 1360 ·

Make pear butter.

· 1361 ·

Use real maple syrup instead of
maple-flavored syrup. (You won't
believe the difference.)

· 1362 ·

Cut wild grapevines and make a wreath.
Put it away to dry until Christmas.

· 1363 ·

Get knee pads and gloves for
working in the garden.

· 1364 ·

Drive down to the marina
and have a long, cool drink
at the dockside café.

· 1365 ·

Walk arm-in-arm with
your sweetie.

· 1366 ·

Order two desserts.

· 1367 ·

Keep in touch by E-mail.

· 1368 ·

Collect all the books
you're finished with and don't want
to keep. Take them to a used book
store and trade them for credit,
so you can pick out more books.

· 1369 ·

Read a novel about someone
your own age.

❀ Do yourself a favor:
If you have unfinished emotional
business with a friend or family member,
it may be time to finish it up
or let it go. Think about it.

· 1371 ·

Invest in yourself—in your dreams,
aspirations, hopes, goals.

· 1372 ·

Fill in your child's baby book
faithfully. Ten or twenty years from
now you'll be glad you did.

· 1373 ·

What was your favorite childhood
sandwich? Bologna? Liverwurst?
Egg salad? Make one today.

· 1374 ·

Stay home on the first day
of a big snow. By the second day the
streets and sidewalks will be cleared
and much easier to negotiate.

· 1375 ·

Keep emergency supplies
in the trunk of your car: blankets,
flashlight, bottle of water, flares,
and whatever else makes good sense
in your part of the country.

· 1376 ·

Wear (fake or real) fur earmuffs
to keep those ears warm.

· 1377 ·

Stash away a few extra blank
audio and video tapes for spur-of-
the-moment recording.

· 1378 ·

Learn to play whatever instrument
you secretly adore.

· 1379 ·

Pamper your hobby by getting
all your supplies nicely organized in
boxes or baskets, on shelves or
pegboard, or in a closet.

· 1380 ·

If you have wonderful art on your walls,
install track lighting to illuminate it.

· 1381 ·

Collect beautiful vases.

· 1382 ·

Buy two bunches of flowers
instead of one.

· 1383 ·

Visit a sensory garden to indulge your
senses of touch, smell, and hearing.

· 1384 ·

Visit a restorative garden to relax
and help your body to heal.

· 1385 ·

Visit a formal garden to enjoy the views.

 Give yourself a break:
Faster is not necessarily better.
Try going slow for a change.

· 1387 ·

Slide into a cold swimming pool inch by
inch instead of plunging right in.

· 1388 ·

Drink chilled sake from a traditional
square wooden box.

· 1389 ·

Read wonderful old travel books.

· 1390 ·

Go to the library and read the
British newspapers for a different
view of everything from politics
to movies to the Royals.

· 1391 ·

Give yourself an electric kettle with
automatic shut-off, to boil water ASAP.

· 1392 ·

Renew your passport the easy
way: by mail.

· 1393 ·

Write out a master packing
list of everything you need for a trip.
Consult it every time you travel.

· 1394 ·

Buy a bonsai tree and make a little
scene beneath it.

· 1395 ·

Sing in the shower.
The acoustics will make
you sound terrific.

· 1396 ·

Track down and nab a couple
of detective films on video:
*L.A. Confidential, Chinatown,
The French Connection,
Devil in a Blue Dress,
The Maltese Falcon, Touch of Evil,
The Pink Panther, Laura,
In the Heat of the Night.*

· 1397 ·

If you and your partner are short on time
spent together, participate (together!)
in something that happens on a regular
basis: a class, lecture or concert series,
workshop, choir, team sport.

· 1398 ·

Buy an easy-pass for driving through
tollbooths without stopping.

· 1399 ·

Get an insulated travel mug to
fill with tea or coffee and take with
you on your daily commute.

· 1400 ·

On a gray winter day, plan
your summer garden.

· 1401 ·

Keep a potpourri in a pretty bowl in
your bedroom, bathroom, or living room.
Stir it occasionally, and add a few drops
of essential oil to perk it up.

· 1402 ·

Put your out-of-season clothes in storage,
so you'll have more room in your closets.

· 1403 ·

Go to a concert of a pop performer
you loved twenty (or more) years ago:
James Taylor, Elton John, Joni Mitchell,
Joan Baez, Rod Stewart, Bruce Springsteen,
Janis Ian, Stevie Wonder.

· 1404 ·

Increase your kitchen storage and work
space with a rolling utility cart that has
shelves and a butcher-block top.

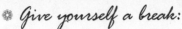

❁ *Give yourself a break:*
If your family is dumping too many
responsibilities on you, call time-out.
Sit down and negotiate a change.

· 1406 ·

Do something fun with your child: baking
cookies, reading, tossing a ball, going to
the zoo, flying a kite, playing Monopoly,
whatever gives pleasure to both of you.

✳ *Call your parents.*

✳ *Don't call your parents.*

· 1409 ·

Place a bouquet of freesia on your
dressing table or night table,
for the delicious fragrance.

· 1410 ·

Ditch the boyfriend who rolls
his eyes and complains that you sound
just like his mother.

· 1411 ·

Keep the guy who loves his mother and
all the rest of his female relatives.

· 1412 ·

Make a collage of family pictures
and keep it on your desk.

· 1413 ·

Relax in a hammock or lawn
chair on a summer evening and
watch the fireflies.

· 1414 ·

Have a cup of sleep-inducing
herbal tea before turning in.

· 1415 ·

Get a sleeping mask.

· 1416 ·

Freeze your Milky Way bar.

· 1417 ·

Make a special excursion to see the
Perseid meteor shower in August.

· 1418 ·

Wear rhinestone earrings, necklace,
bracelet, and sparkle like a star.

· 1419 ·

Attend a film festival.

· 1420 ·

Redecorate your office.

· 1421 ·

Have a tag sale to clear out the attic—
and make a little dough.

· 1422 ·

Rekindle a friendship you used
to enjoy but have allowed to cool.

· 1423 ·

Apply to grad school.

· 1424 ·

Go to a brew pub and have a
glass of freshly made beer.

· 1425 ·

Call for take-out food when
friends come to dinner.

· 1426 ·

Bake brownies.

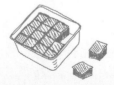

· 1427 ·

Spend six months traveling in Europe.

· 1428 ·

Spend a week at a spa.

· 1429 ·

Buy the hardcover instead
of the paperback.

· 1430 ·

Replace all those ugly drawer pulls and
doorknobs you've always hated.

 Do yourself a favor:
Let go of the fantasy that someday you'll
want to wear that weird purple and yellow
dress. Now let go of the dress.

· 1432 ·

Before you leave for the airport, call your
airline to be sure the flight is on time.

· 1433 ·

Get a bigger TV.

· 1434 ·

Have your favorite chair reupholstered
in a fabric you absolutely adore.

· 1435 ·

Hire a professional
matchmaker.

· 1436 ·

Have your wedding invitations handwritten
by a professional calligrapher.

· 1437 ·

Learn the basics of yoga breathing,
then do it often.

· 1438 ·

Go to sports camp for a week.

· 1439 ·

Ask your grandmother to patch
your cherished flannel shirt.

· 1440 ·

Teach your favorite childhood songs
to your own children.

· 1441 ·

Order an ice cream cake for
your birthday.

· 1442 ·

If you can afford it, contribute
money to a cause you believe in;
if you can't, donate a little time.

❋ *Give yourself a break:*
In a tough situation, follow your instincts.
Even if things don't work out, you'll have
done what you think is right.

· 1444 ·

Ask your movie date
to tell you when the scary or violent
part is over, so you can take your
hands away from your eyes and
your fingers out of your ears.

· 1445 ·

If you're blue and you need pampering,
ask a friend to stay overnight at your
house and keep you company.

· 1446 ·

Have a deck built.

· 1447 ·

Have a porch built.

· 1448 ·

Have a patio laid.

· 1449 ·

Buy really good ground beef
for your hamburgers.

· 1450 ·

Switch to nonstick skillets
for almost instant cleanup.
You'll cut down on fat too.

· 1451 ·

Buy a thermal carafe to keep
liquids piping hot or icy cold.

· 1452 ·

Invite your brothers and sisters to
a Siblings Party. Tell stories about
each other, look at old pictures, eat the
foods you loved when you were kids.

· 1453 ·

Decorate a dollhouse.

· 1454 ·

Skip rocks on a glassy lake.

· 1455 ·

Make a terrarium.

· 1456 ·

Build a snowperson.

· 1457 ·

Make blondies.

· 1458 ·

Jump rope.

✳ *Go on the roller coaster.*

✳ *Don't go on the roller coaster.*

· 1461 ·

Ride a limo to the airport instead of
taking the airport shuttle bus.

· 1462 ·

Hike the boulder-strewn beach at
La Push and the rain forest in Olympic
National Park in northern Washington.

· 1463 ·

Visit a chocolate factory
and taste, taste, taste.

· 1464 ·

Buy more panty hose than
you need today, so you don't have
to do it again tomorrow.

· 1465 ·

Have an Alfred Hitchcock Video
Festival in the privacy of your own home:
Rent *Rear Window, North by Northwest,
Vertigo, The Birds, Marnie*

· 1466 ·

Throw yourself a milestone-birthday
bash. That's the way to get the
party you really want.

· 1467 ·

Identify yourself: Have towels
or sheets monogrammed.

· 1468 ·

Have a BLT with enough mayo.

· 1469 ·

Learn to roller-blade.

· 1470 ·

Sit down in a field of daffodils, a rolling sea
of brilliant yellow and rich green.

· 1471 ·

Leave work early on the day
before a holiday.

· 1472 ·

Lounge around in a steam room.

· 1473 ·

Have a picnic in bed.

· 1474 ·

When you're feeling grumpy around
the edges, sit down and make a list
of your personal best things-that-
money-can't-buy. Think hard.
You'll be surprised at how many there are.

· 1475 ·

Get a shower radio.

· 1476 ·

Go out for an Early Bird Special dinner.

· 1477 ·

Send an unsigned valentine to your secret love—and then let the object of your affection know you sent it.

❀ *Give yourself a break:*
If a casual acquaintance starts telling you more personal information than you want to know, stop her. You're *not* required to listen.

· 1479 ·

Punctuate a day of boring errands and chores with treats: cappuccino at a café, a trip to the library, buying new makeup, a box of buttered popcorn.

· 1480 ·

Go to a service at a church famous for a particular kind of music— gospel, brass, organ, folk.

· 1481 ·

Be awed by the Lincoln Memorial
in Washington, D.C.

· 1482 ·

When life gives you lemons, make lemonade.

❀ *Do yourself a favor:*
Don't do everything yourself. Delegate.

· 1484 ·

Let the family pamper you just
because you need pampering.

· 1485 ·

Go to a friend's house for dinner
and *don't* help with the dishes.

· 1486 ·

Stop, look, and listen: *Stop* rushing here and
there like a maniac. *Look* around you. *Listen*
to what's really going on in your head.

· 1487 ·

Scout around for someone you think
would be a good career mentor. Take
her to lunch and pick her brain.

· 1488 ·

Hire an office planner to design
your home office.

· 1489 ·

Have a computer consultant
come to your home to upgrade your
software, set up your new printer,
transfer information to your laptop.

· 1490 ·

Get yourself an office chair that's
ergonomically designed and
supercomfortable.

· 1491 ·

Treat yourself to a battery-operated
pencil sharpener.

· 1492 ·

Put neatly printed or typed new
labels on all your file folders.

❀ *Give yourself a break:*
Declare an off-season Mother's Day.

· 1494 ·

Throw a party for your coworkers
so *they* will know you appreciate them—
and *you* will reap the benefits on the job.

· 1495 ·

Honor your nourishing, enriching
friendships. Firmly disengage from
destructive ones.

· 1496 ·

Buy a chocolate bar made with chocolate
produced by a cooperative in South
America and feel virtuous instead of guilty.

· 1497 ·

Start a retirement account.

· 1498 ·

Subscribe to a literary magazine.

· 1499 ·

Sit in a porch swing and spend
the evening dreaming.

· 1500 ·

Have a "Night of the Star": Watch videos—
lots of them—of your all-time favorite actor.

· 1501 ·

Hold hands with
your beloved.

· 1502 ·
Make apple fritters.

· 1503 ·
Make a list of the books
you want to read and check them
off as you finish them.

· 1504 ·
Stop struggling to reach those
high shelves: Get yourself a stepstool
or a small stepladder.

· 1505 ·
Keep basic baking staples on hand,
so you can whip up a batch of cookies
whenever you want to.

· 1506 ·
Keep five twenty-dollar bills in a secret
place, so you'll feel secure.

· 1507 ·
Make chicken soup from scratch.

· 1508 ·
Wear really warm socks.

· 1509 ·
In summer, stock up on sunscreen,

 so you'll never be caught
without it on a
wonderful beach day.

· 1510 ·
In winter, stock up on medication,
cough drops, tissues, so you'll be
prepared when you get the flu.

· 1511 ·
If dry winter air makes
you itchy and congested, get a
humidifier and feel better fast.

· 1512 ·

Instead of going out in the cold or
rain for a video, dial pay-TV.

· 1513 ·

Wrap up in a pure mohair throw
on a chilly night.

· 1514 ·

Hire someone to shovel your paths
and driveway after a big snow.

· 1515 ·

Fall asleep on the couch, snuggled
up to your sweetheart.

· 1516 ·

Try honey in your coffee instead of sugar.

· 1517 ·

Invest in a great omelet pan.

· 1518 ·

Have crispy brown homefries
with your eggs.

· 1519 ·

Establish a morning routine,
so you don't have to think each day about
what to do and when to do it.

· 1520 ·

To increase your chances of a good, sound
sleep, develop a quiet, soothing bedtime
routine that you repeat each night.

· 1521 ·

Dress up and take binoculars
to the opera. Drink champagne
in the intermission.

· 1522 ·

Make a transcontinental phone call.

· 1523 ·
Join a food co-op.

· 1524 ·
Let your partner carry the groceries.

· 1525 ·
Peel the apple before eating it.

· 1526 ·
Swipe the last piece of chocolate cake.

· 1527 ·
When you're feeling poor and
downtrodden, volunteer at a
soup kitchen for a day.

❧ *Do yourself a favor:*
Stop saving your possessions
or your clothes for a special occasion.
Life is right now.

· 1529 ·

If you're lonely, make a date.
Don't wait to be called.

· 1530 ·

Entertain with a Sunday brunch:
The food is easy to prepare, you can serve
it buffet style, and you'll have the whole
evening for cleanup. And you'll be rested
and perky for work on Monday.

· 1531 ·

Keep a wonderful secret to yourself.

· 1532 ·

Hang a key holder near the
door you use most, so you'll stop
misplacing your keys.

· 1533 ·

Put up a full-length mirror.

· 1534 ·

Install a light in your clothes closet.

· 1535 ·

Play your favorite childhood game:
jacks, pick-up-sticks, cat's cradle,
tag, hide-and-seek.

· 1536 ·

Indulge in petits fours—those pretty little
cakes made of genoise, jam, and a thick
icing. Can you ever get enough?

· 1537 ·

Dress up and go to a chic
cabaret or nightclub.

· 1538 ·

Pin a gardenia to your party dress and
smell like a dream. It's magic!

· 1539 ·
Plan a trip you can actually afford.
Set a date and *go*.

· 1540 ·
Install good lighting around the mirror
you use when you put on makeup.

· 1541 ·
Take off your clothes in
a sunny, secluded meadow. Feel the
sun on *all* of your skin.

· 1542 ·
See spring in Chicago. Visit Grant Park,
the Field Museum, the Navy Pier. Take a
boat tour and view the architectural
treasures of a great city.

· 1543 ·
Remodel your bathroom.

· 1544 ·

Let the liquor store deliver the goods
when you're throwing a party.

· 1545 ·

Reciprocate dinner invitations
by taking your friends out for a meal,
instead of cooking at home.

· 1546 ·

Redecorate for the changing seasons:
Replace heavy slipcovers, pillow shams,
and bedspreads with light ones, dark
colors with pale ones.

· 1547 ·

Buy *comfortable* patio furniture.

· 1548 ·

Cook a shore dinner over a
fire on the beach.

· 1549 ·

Visit a flower show to revel
in the colors and fragrances,
and to get a few ideas for
your own garden.

· 1550 ·

Play with an infant,
then give him back to his
parents and be glad your own
infants are grown.

· 1551 ·

Find a partner who shares
the housework equally.
Without being told.

· 1552 ·

Let your cat comfort you
when you're sad.

· 1553 ·

Sit on the edge of your sofa with courtroom dramas on video: *True Believer, And Justice for All, Philadelphia, The Verdict, The Caine Mutiny, Inherit the Wind, Witness for the Prosecution.*

✻ *Do your shopping on the Internet.*

✻ *Don't do your shopping on the Internet.*

· 1556 ·

Stop yearning for things you can't afford.

· 1557 ·

Lie in a field of summer grass and be so quiet that insects and butterflies forget you're there. Inhale the dry, green scent. Think about nothing.

· 1558 ·

Write your own children's
book and illustrate it with your
own drawings or photos.

· 1559 ·

Be spontaneous.

· 1560 ·

Let your imagination run wild.

· 1561 ·

Try a fancy mixed drink—
a Cosmopolitan, Pimm's cup,
Rob Roy, Singapore sling.

· 1562 ·

When friends are coming for
dinner, say yes when they offer
to bring wine or dessert.

· 1563 ·

Enlist your new teenaged
driver to do all the chores
that require driving.

· 1564 ·

Make sure your car's spare tire
is in good condition.

· 1565 ·

Get a back support for your car seat,
so driving is more comfortable.

❀ *Do yourself a favor:*
When you have to lift or pick up
something, bend from the knees—
never from the hips.

· 1567 ·

Install slide-out shelves, drawers,
or wire baskets in low cabinets, so
you can reach the contents easily.

· 1568 ·

Get one of those zippered personal organizers meant for travel, the kind that hangs on the back of the hotel bathroom door. Use it in your bathroom at home to hold down the clutter.

· 1569 ·

Invest in a self-cleaning oven.

· 1570 ·

Have you been taught to be a neat freak? Try being messy.

· 1571 ·

Have you been taught never to lose your temper? Try getting mad.

· 1572 ·

Have you been taught to put others first? Try putting yourself first.

· 1573 ·

Turn up the heat, so you'll be
really warm.

· 1574 ·

Eat only your favorite foods for a week.

· 1575 ·

Wear your old charm bracelet.

· 1576 ·

Write your autobiography.

· 1577 ·

Say what you really mean.

· 1578 ·

Take a trip by yourself.

· 1579 ·

Buy a one-cup cone and one-cup
filters for brewing fresh drip coffee
right in your coffee cup.

· 1580 ·

Have your favorite dress
(or slacks or blouse) copied by a good
dressmaker, in a flattering fabric.

· 1581 ·

Give yourself a brand-new
hardcover of a much-read,
dog-eared favorite paperback.

· 1582 ·

Get a wireless intercom for tuning in or
talking anywhere in the house.

· 1583 ·

Retreat from the world for a
few days, to replenish, revive,
recuperate, recover, recharge,
refresh, regenerate, renew.

· 1584 ·

Do something repetitious and soothing:
pet a cat, rock in a rocker, crochet,
jog, shell peas, brush your hair.

· 1585 ·

Have a love affair.

· 1586 ·

Plan your future together.

· 1587 ·

Give an election night party,
so you can celebrate (or commiserate)
in good company.

❂ *Give yourself a break:*
Don't answer questions that are too
personal, too nosy, too ridiculous.

· 1589 ·
Eat your favorite junk food without
feeling guilty—just this once.

· 1590 ·
Clean out that catch-all drawer
in the kitchen.

· 1591 ·
Eat a snack of ripe pear wedges, creamy
Brie, crisp crackers, and toasted pecans.

· 1592 ·
Buy yourself a gift certificate to your
local beauty salon, and save it up for a day
when you need special pampering.

· 1593 ·
Treat yourself to half a dozen
miniature fruit tartlets.

· 1594 ·

Hire someone to cook for
your next big dinner party. And
someone to clean up too.

· 1595 ·

Turn off the electric lights
and spend an evening in
romantic candlelight.

· 1596 ·

Take a real lunch break:
Use your lunch hour to do
something interesting that's
unrelated to your work.

❀ *Give yourself a break:*
Remember that each day you can
probably accomplish only a quarter
of what you wish you could.

· 1598 ·

If you're perpetually harried and
interrupted at home or in the office,
pick out two hours of each day when you
don't answer the phone.

· 1599 ·

When you hear the call of
the wild, answer it.

· 1600 ·

Bet the farm on a video about gambling:
*Paper Moon, The Color of Money,
The Sting, The Hustler, The Lady Eve,
Kansas City, Casino.*

· 1601 ·

Wear something sexy: tight,
sheer, low-cut, satin, leather,
leopard-printed, high-heeled—whatever
works for the two of you.

· 1602 ·

Invite your sweetheart on a ride
through the Tunnel of Love.

· 1603 ·

Figure out how much cash you need this
week and make only *one* trip to the ATM.

· 1604 ·

Buy a pair of glittery dancing shoes.

· 1605 ·

Learn to dive.

· 1606 ·

Have your martini in a
real martini glass, chilled
in the fridge or freezer.

· 1607 ·

Get home safely.

· 1608 ·
Congratulate yourself on
any job well done.

· 1609 ·
Decide not to be a victim.

· 1610 ·
Take a class in self-defense.

· 1611 ·
Leave your bed unmade for a day.

· 1612 ·
Fire the inner critic who tells you what
you're doing wrong, and hire the one who
tells you what you're doing right.

· 1613 ·
Let go of your compulsive
behavior.

· 1614 ·

Wear flowing clothes that float
around you romantically.

· 1615 ·

Wear clingy clothes that show
off your good figure.

· 1616 ·

Wear stretchy clothes that move
with you and don't bind.

❀ *Do yourself a favor:*
Bend, don't break.

· 1618 ·

Can't finish all your work today?
Don't stay late at the office.
Make an executive decision
to finish it tomorrow.

· 1619 ·

Pull your armchair over to
the window, tuck an afghan around
your legs, and daydream.

· 1620 ·

Read a few of the Great Books
you missed in high school:
Emma by Jane Austen,
Jane Eyre by Charlotte Brontë,
Huckleberry Finn by Mark Twain,
David Copperfield by Charles Dickens.

· 1621 ·

If you love freshly brewed tea, treat
yourself to a chubby little brown
Rockingham teapot—the real
thing, from England.

· 1622 ·

Buy an old-fashioned cookie jar
and keep it filled.

· 1623 ·

Visit vintage shops and tag sales to collect
embroidered tea towels. Use them every day.

· 1624 ·

Make "bread" pudding from leftover plain cake.

· 1625 ·

Bring back a family tradition that has
somehow fallen by the wayside.

· 1626 ·

At long last, get yourself a good, big turkey
platter. Try yard sales for a bargain.

· 1627 ·

Replace the missing pieces in your set
of china, crystal, or flatware.

· 1628 ·
Every time you shop for groceries,
buy one interesting new item
or one *favorite* item.

· 1629 ·
Organize your recipe cards, so you can find
the one you want when you want it.

· 1630 ·
Take a spiral walk around the
Boston Aquarium.

· 1631 ·
Clean out your jewelry box and give
away what you don't wear anymore,
to make room for new goodies.

· 1632 ·
Hire a carpenter or cabinetmaker to
build in as much storage as you need.

· 1633 ·

Buy yourself that coffee table book
you've been drooling over.

· 1634 ·

Get a group together around a piano and
let loose on all your favorite songs.

 Watch the football game.

✳ *Don't watch the football game.*

· 1637 ·

Go outside and play.

· 1638 ·

Eat chocolate sauce from the jar.

· 1639 ·

Use your Frequent Flyer
miles for an upgrade.

· 1640 ·
Clean out your handbag.

· 1641 ·
Save up for a suede jacket.

· 1642 ·
Decorate your house with lace:
curtains, tablecloths, bedspreads,
dust ruffle, runners, pillows.

· 1643 ·
In spring, buy
a huge bunch of
lilacs the minute they
arrive at your local florist.

· 1644 ·
When you're beset by nostalgia,
hang out for an afternoon in
your old neighborhood.

❀ *Give yourself a break:*
Make peace with your demons.

· 1646 ·
Just say "no."

· 1647 ·
Just say "yes."

· 1648 ·
Just say "maybe later."

· 1649 ·
Stop and listen to pealing bells,
a sidewalk quartet, a street musician,
a splashing fountain, people speaking
a foreign language, music from
an open window.

· 1650 ·
Fly down a frosty hill on a snow saucer.

· 1651 ·
Button up your overcoat, put on your
hat and scarf, and pull on your gloves
before you go out in the cold.

· 1652 ·
Put an extra blanket at the foot of
your bed, so you don't have to get up to
find one in the middle of the night.

· 1653 ·
Make a yummy hot toddy:
Combine two jiggers of dark rum, a twist
of lemon peel, a clove, and a cinnamon
stick in a mug. Add boiling cider and float
a small pat of butter on top.

· 1654 ·
Ask your partner to tuck you into bed.

· 1655 ·

Top your breakfast cereal with fruit: raisins, bananas, blueberries, strawberries, or peaches.

· 1656 ·

Warm the coffee cake before you eat it.
Delicious.

· 1657 ·

Instead of bolting down lunch at your desk, take it to the park and cool out away from the office, alone or with a friend.

· 1658 ·

Overwhelmed? Hire a personal assistant for a day or a week.

❀ *Do yourself a favor:*

Use the buddy system for getting big chores done. Help a friend clean out her closet this weekend, and she helps you clean out your mudroom next weekend.

· 1660 ·

Buy a second vacuum cleaner and
keep it on the second floor of your
house so you can stop lugging a single
vacuum up and down stairs.

· 1661 ·

Stock up on extra bags for
your vacuum cleaner.

· 1662 ·

Keep gourmet frozen dinners
on hand for easy meals.

· 1663 ·

Have a juicy steak and a baked potato.

· 1664 ·

Program your VCR to record
your favorite TV show when you can't
be home to watch it.

· 1665 ·

Pick up a horseshoe-shaped
travel pillow to use on planes or
trains, to avoid a stiff neck.

· 1666 ·

Get on a night flight, take a sleeping pill,
and wake up at your destination.

· 1667 ·

Explore the unknown with adventure
books: *Mutiny on the Bounty,
Stones for Ibarra, The Scarlet Pimpernel,
Into Thin Air, Lord of the Flies.*

· 1668 ·

Attend a department store fashion
show to get new wardrobe ideas.

· 1669 ·
If you don't like the gift you've been given,
exchange it for something
you really want.

· 1670 ·
Visit the Museum of International Folk
Art in Santa Fe, New Mexico.

❀ *Give yourself a break:*
Allot at least an hour each day for doing
something that gives you pleasure.

· 1672 ·
Take a nap.

· 1673 ·
Walk in a deeply silent pine forest.

· 1674 ·
Make a rock garden.

· 1675 ·
Play the jukebox as much as you want.

· 1676 ·
Play kissing games—Spin-the-Bottle
or Post Office, for instance.

· 1677 ·
Stock your bar.

· 1678 ·
Treat yourself to a bathroom
scale with l-a-r-g-e numbers
you can see easily.

· 1679 ·
Let your lover take you
out to dinner.

· 1680 ·
Make fresh orange juice.

· 1681 ·

Buy champagne flutes.

· 1682 ·

Take a (quiet) brown bag lunch
to an afternoon movie.

· 1683 ·

Eat vanilla ice cream with fresh berries.

· 1684 ·

Kick off your shoes and dangle
your feet in the pond.

· 1685 ·

Rent videos of films you loved as a kid:
The Red Shoes, Mary Poppins,
The Wizard of Oz, ET, Star Wars.

· 1686 ·

Spend a rainy afternoon in Wisconsin eating
Cheddar and salami at a cheese factory.

· 1687 ·
Take a party boat ride.

· 1688 ·
Go mountain biking in Utah.

· 1689 ·
Get a good sturdy shopping
cart for transporting groceries,
packages, laundry to and fro.

· 1690 ·
Treat yourself to a classic garment
from a good retail store.

· 1691 ·
Buy an electric towel warmer
to heat your bath towel while
you relax in the tub.

· 1692 ·
Build a campfire. Toast marshmallows.

· 1693 ·
Vacation at a dude ranch.

· 1694 ·
Declare a fence-mending week,
and patch up the broken relationships
(with family, friends, lovers)
you've been trying to ignore.

· 1695 ·
For a private cry, hop into the shower,
where no one will hear you and the
water will wash away your tears.

· 1696 ·
Smuggle your favorite snacks
into the movie theater.

· 1697 ·
Get yourself a portable CD player and
a case for carrying your favorite discs.

· 1698 ·

Zone out for an hour or two playing
handheld electronic games.

· 1699 ·

Use your calculator instead of your fingers
when you're balancing your checkbook.

❀ *Do yourself a favor:*

Don't take on more than you can handle.

· 1701 ·

If your collection of antique mechanical
banks or Dresden shepherdesses is getting
out of hand or boring, stop collecting.

· 1702 ·

Spend a weekend afternoon with your
significant other: Browse in stores, have
a delicious snack, go to the movies, and
finish the day with a good dinner.

· 1703 ·

Make a batch of fudge.

· 1704 ·

Photograph the great
moments of your life.

· 1705 ·

Put your snapshots in a good-looking
album so you can enjoy them
anytime you like.

· 1706 ·

Read an interesting travel
book and daydream about the
trips you might take.

· 1707 ·

Have chilled red or white gazpacho
on a hot summer day, with a glass of cold
wine and a loaf of fresh bread.

· 1708 ·

Put your cat on your tummy when you have
cramps. Pet her so she'll purr
your pain away.

· 1709 ·

Dry your hair by the fire.

· 1710 ·

Wear long, loungy dresses at home,
for a feeling of elegance and ease.

· 1711 ·

Make a bouquet of silk flowers.

· 1712 ·

Invest in fine-quality sports equipment.

· 1713 ·

Buy a rolling carry-on bag for
business and other trips, so you don't
have to lug your luggage.

· 1714 ·
Have a fruit smoothie for energy
in the late afternoon.

· 1715 ·
If you travel a lot, keep ready a
zippered case of essentials: toothbrush
and -paste, shampoo, deodorant,
comb and brush, aspirin, etc.

· 1716 ·
Get really solid advice before investing
a penny. Consult a *proven* expert
before buying stocks or bonds.

· 1717 ·
Use long-life lightbulbs.

· 1718 ·
When you're too busy (or too tired)
to make a delivery yourself, call a
messenger service.

· 1719 ·

Soothe and massage your tired feet
with a hydrotherapeutic foot spa.

· 1720 ·

Slow down. Don't rush. Walk instead of ride.
Take the local instead of the express. Follow
a leisurely, roundabout route instead of the
shortest distance between two points.

 Give yourself a break:
Excuse yourself and walk out of a bad
situation, whether it's a fight, a party,
a movie, or a meeting.

· 1722 ·

Ask your partner to kiss it
and make it better.

· 1723 ·

Make your bedroom a romantic place—
gentle lighting, soft fabrics, warm colors.

· 1724 ·

Hang herbal sachets in your closet.

· 1725 ·

Lie under a leafy tree and observe the
sun and sky through the canopy.

· 1726 ·

Watch workout shows and
don't work out.

· 1727 ·

Take the time to find jeans
that fit perfectly.

· 1728 ·

Buy prewashed lettuce mixes for salads.

· 1729 ·

Buy a water filter that attaches
to your kitchen faucet or fits
onto a special pitcher.

· 1730 ·
Slip a mattress board between your
old mattress and box spring for
increased firmness and comfort.

· 1731 ·
Get into the drama of videotaped films
about entertainment: *The King of Comedy,*
The Turning Point, The Entertainer,
All That Jazz, Fame, All About Eve,
The Sweet Smell of Success,
Singing in the Rain.

· 1732 ·
Eat fresh figs in season.

❀ *Do yourself a favor:*
Stop worrying about your weight.

· 1734 ·
Wear your good jewelry often.

· 1735 ·
Replace the heels on your
rundown shoes.

· 1736 ·
Need more storage? Over-the-door
racks with hooks or shelves
require no installation.

· 1737 ·
Hire a hardworking teenager to
help you clean out your garage.

· 1738 ·
Spend a summer afternoon under
a shady tree, with friends and a pitcher
of chilled homemade sangria.

· 1739 ·

Buy yourself a flowering plant
in the dead of winter.

· 1740 ·

Get a group of friends together for
an evening of informal play-reading.
Try comedy, tragedy, drama, or farce—
anything from *Romeo and Juliet* to *Cat
on a Hot Tin Roof* to *The Odd Couple*.

 Give yourself a break:
Let somebody else baby-sit the kids
at the family party for a change.

· 1742 ·

Let your partner take a snooze with
his head resting on your lap.

· 1743 ·

Buy a leather couch or chair.

· 1744 ·

Order a club sandwich.

· 1745 ·

Give yourself the baseball mitt you always
wanted when you were a kid.

· 1746 ·

Use book plates or an embossing
stamper to identify your books, so
they'll be returned to you.

· 1747 ·

If the restaurant food is great and
you can't finish it all, take it home with
you for a terrific lunch tomorrow.

· 1748 ·

Do something special after work:
concert, movie, lecture, sports event,
poetry reading, theater.

· 1749 ·

Play charades.

· 1750 ·

Stretch your mind with word puzzles—
crosswords, crostics, and cryptics.

· 1751 ·

Have your knives sharpened by a real pro.

· 1752 ·

Learn to carve a chicken.

❀ *Give yourself a break:*
Don't try to accomplish your big goal in
one giant step. Break it down into smaller
steps and take them one by one.

· 1754 ·

Have a package of dark chocolate
thin mints all for yourself.

· 1755 ·

Toss out that tattered tote bag and treat
yourself to a really good-looking new one.

· 1756 ·

Request a premium brand instead of the
bar brand when you have a drink.

· 1757 ·

Order the special-of-the-day.

· 1758 ·

If the sun and the breeze and the
blue sky beckon you, drop what you're
doing and go out to meet them.

· 1759 ·

When you're traveling, travel light.

· 1760 ·

If you know you're going to have to move
house in six months or a year, start clearing
out the attic and basement *now*.

· 1761 ·
Flirt as much as you want at the
next party you go to.

 Do yourself a favor:
Share your fears and anxieties
with a trustworthy friend.

· 1763 ·
Grant yourself permission to
speak up against unfairness and speak
out against injustice.

· 1764 ·
Give yourself a reward for getting
through a horrible day.

· 1765 ·
Hide behind wraparound sunglasses
and under a big hat.

· 1766 ·
Go to a playground
and ride on the swings,
the seesaw,
the roundabout.

· 1767 ·
Eat the wontons
and leave the soup.

· 1768 ·
Have a Plan B in case
Plan A doesn't work.

· 1769 ·
Spend more time alone.

· 1770 ·
Spend less time alone.

· 1771 ·
Have a marzipan fruit. Have two.

· 1772 ·

Hire a professional to paint your apartment.

· 1773 ·

Indulge in ruffles: dust ruffle on your bed,
ruffles on your curtains, ruffles on your
skirt, ruffles at the neck of your blouse.

· 1774 ·

Accept compliments so graciously that the
giver will be eager to pay you another one.

· 1775 ·

Use butter instead of margarine.

· 1776 ·

Eat all the chunky blue cheese
dressing you want.

· 1777 ·

Bring a bottle of your favorite wine
to your favorite restaurant.

· 1778 ·

Spend a whole day doing *exactly*
what you feel like doing.

 Get into an argument.

 Don't get into an argument.

· 1781 ·

Laugh too loud.

· 1782 ·

Kiss and make up.

· 1783 ·

When the party's really
hopping, stay late.

· 1784 ·

Walk barefoot
in the rain.
Squish your toes in the mud puddles.

· 1785 ·

Drop the fad diet and start eating sensibly.

· 1786 ·

Let your face breathe for a day:
Don't put on makeup.

· 1787 ·

Clip, tie, tuck, or braid your hair
with pretty ornaments.

 Do yourself a favor:
If you hate to be alone on Saturday
night, make plans.

· 1789 ·

Go to a tapas bar and try all the
little dishes on the menu, accompanied
by a glass of good sherry.

· 1790 ·

Get a corkscrew that's easy to use.

· 1791 ·
Have your kitchen cabinets
refinished.

· 1792 ·
Paint a mural on your wall.

· 1793 ·
Take good care of your
family heirlooms.

· 1794 ·
Set your house in order.

· 1795 ·
Don't miss the January sales.

· 1796 ·
If someone gives you an unexpected
present, don't feel guilty or unworthy.
You're being pampered!

· 1797 ·

Let your sweetheart know that you want
something special for Valentine's Day.

· 1798 ·

Enjoy looking at expensive art
books in a good bookstore.

· 1799 ·

Order filet mignon by mail.

· 1800 ·

If you can't have a full-fledged grill on
your balcony, get a hibachi instead.

· 1801 ·

Make chocolate fondue and dunk fresh
strawberries and squares of pound cake.

❋ *Join a gym.*

❋ *Don't join a gym.*

· 1804 ·

Wear a flower in your hair.

· 1805 ·

Dance to the music you danced
to in high school.

· 1806 ·

Celebrate your wedding anniversary in a
romantic way, just the two of you.

· 1807 ·

Celebrate your wedding anniversary with
a huge party for family and friends.

· 1808 ·

Sail on a luxury liner.

· 1809 ·

Make a promise to yourself about your goals, your career, your relationships, or whatever is most important to you— and try to keep it.

· 1810 ·

Arrive at an agreement with your partner: You'll spend one night a week apart, out with your pals, doing something your partner doesn't enjoy—bowling, going to the theater, eating sushi, attending a book group, and so on.

· 1811 ·

Hike to the farthest easterly point of Long Island, New York, right under the Montauk Lighthouse.

· 1812 ·

Make a list and do errands only once a week.

· 1813 ·

Buy yourself a whole box of manila file
folders so you never run out.

❁ *Give yourself a break:*
Treat yourself as well as you'd
treat a dear friend.

· 1815 ·

Wear rubber gloves when you wash
dishes or clean *anything.*

· 1816 ·

Buy a long-term pass for commuter
trains or public transit, so you
don't have to wait in line.

· 1817 ·

Store things where you use them.

· 1818 ·

Walk away from people who dwell
obsessively on the negative.

· 1819 ·

Have your eyebrows shaped and
dyed professionally.

· 1820 ·

Wear bright, cheerful clothes when
you're feeling gloomy.

· 1821 ·

Wear dark, soulful clothes when
you're feeling gloomy.

· 1822 ·

Do not starve yourself in order to
have a flat stomach.

· 1823 ·

Sit on a big rock and watch a stream
or river flow. Think about how life—
like the stream—is never the same
from moment to moment.

· 1824 ·
Start writing a journal.

· 1825 ·
Cultivate friendships.

· 1826 ·
Find a reliable travel agent.

· 1827 ·
Treat yourself to an electric mixer.

· 1828 ·
Make popovers.

· 1829 ·
Rent a summer house.

· 1830 ·
Hire a professional pool person to
maintain your swimming pool.

· 1831 ·
Have hors d'oeuvres for dinner—
at a restaurant, from a take-out place,
or even the frozen variety.

· 1832 ·
Take tennis lessons.

· 1833 ·
Eat cake batter.

· 1834 ·
Snuggle with your sweetie.

· 1835 ·
When you're low on energy, kick back
and watch a video action film:
Raiders of the Lost Ark,
Lethal Weapon, Dirty Harry, Speed,
The Fugitive.

· 1836 ·

If you absolutely have to move, have the
(reliable) movers do the packing too.

✳ *Procrastinate.*

✳ *Don't procrastinate.*

· 1839 ·

Use travel downtime on planes, trains,
buses for reading something you've
been looking forward to.

· 1840 ·

Ask for a window seat on the plane,
so you can watch the view.

· 1841 ·

Ask for an aisle seat on the plane,
so you can get up without having to
ask someone to move.

· 1842 ·

Treat yourself to personalized notepads.

· 1843 ·

Learn desktop publishing.

· 1844 ·

Work at your own speed.

· 1845 ·

Where love is concerned, get what
you need by asking for it.

· 1846 ·

Cut up a ripe pineapple.
Bite into it and let the juice run
down your chin.

· 1847 ·

Put a spiffy new
lampshade on your
favorite base.

· 1848 ·

Take a carriage ride around the park.

· 1849 ·

Eat hot biscuits with butter and honey.

· 1850 ·

Have an artist paint a
portrait of your pet.

· 1851 ·

Wander through the Winterthur
Museum in Wilmington, Delaware,
for a taste of colonial America.

· 1852 ·

Buy new underwear.

· 1853 ·

Always carry a pair of earplugs,
for instant silence.

· 1854 ·
Try contact lenses.

· 1855 ·
Finish your work quickly and have
time to do something fun.

· 1856 ·
Join the crowds in a city park for
group sledding on a frosty day.

· 1857 ·
Read the book, then see the movie.

· 1858 ·
Wear a sexy negligee.

· 1859 ·
Loosen up and revise
your plans.

❀ *Give yourself a break:*
Instead of baking a scratch cake for that
birthday party or bake sale, make it from
a mix or buy it at the bakery.

· 1861 ·
Order birthday presents by mail,
and have them delivered to the
intended recipients.

· 1862 ·
Buy yourself a filing cabinet
and get organized.

· 1863 ·
Get a bigger handbag.

· 1864 ·
Make tea sandwiches: watercress and
smoked salmon, date-nut bread with cream
cheese, chopped egg and cucumber.

· 1865 ·

Get a belt rack and a tie rack
for your closet.

· 1866 ·

Do you know someone who
accomplishes a lot? Ask her to
teach you her techniques.

❀ *Do yourself a favor:*
When the going gets tough, consider
abandoning ship. It may be better
for you in the long run.

· 1868 ·

Pay a visit to the old-style seaport
in Mystic, Connecticut.

· 1869 ·

Give yourself a "Bon Voyage" party
before you leave on a trip.

· 1870 ·
Munch on chocolate-covered
coffee beans.

· 1871 ·
Suck on a honeycomb.

· 1872 ·
Plant bulbs in autumn, so you'll have
a glorious display in spring.

❋ *Make dyed, decorated
Easter eggs.*

❋ *Don't make dyed, decorated
Easter eggs.*

· 1875 ·
Have a bowl of kids' cereal:
Fruit Loops, Lucky Charms,
Apple Jacks, Cap'n Crunch.

· 1876 ·

Sleep with your stuffed animals
clutched to your chest.

· 1877 ·

Cuddle with your partner late at
night or early in the morning.

· 1878 ·

Go ballroom dancing in a full skirt.

· 1879 ·

Break the rules.

· 1880 ·

Hire out as crew on a tall ship
for an afternoon.

· 1881 ·

Make a phone call from
an airplane.

· 1882 ·

Sit by a pond on a
summer night and listen
to the frogs.

· 1883 ·

Eat as many baked clams
as you want.

· 1884 ·

Take along a mother's helper or
baby-sitter when you go out for
dinner with the children.

· 1885 ·

Put an extra towel rack in the bathroom.

· 1886 ·

Buy a pretty apron.

· 1887 ·

Start a reading club.

· 1888 ·

Study with a group of friends.

· 1889 ·

Hire someone to type your report,
thesis, term paper, novel.

· 1890 ·

Remember that huge pile of
magazines you've been meaning to read?
Throw it away.

❀ *Give yourself a break:*
Be generous to yourself.

· 1892 ·

Don't wear skirts or dresses
with dowdy hemlines. Take them up,
let them down, or have a tailor
do it for you.

· 1893 ·

If your absolutely favorite wool blanket
or sweater contracts a case of moth holes,
treat yourself to a reweaving job.

· 1894 ·

In snow country, put on a few pairs of
pants and go sledding without the sled.

· 1895 ·

Prepare homemade ice cream.

· 1896 ·

Wear seriously warm gloves
in cold weather.

· 1897 ·

Ask your partner to sleep in the
guest room or on the living room couch
when you're suffering with the flu.

· 1898 ·

Wear your lover's well-used T-shirt
when he's away and you're alone.

· 1899 ·

Treat yourself to a compact lap desk
so you can write with convenience
on sofa, in your favorite armchair,
or on the commuter train.

· 1900 ·

Furnish a room with unpainted furniture
painted *your* way—bright colors, stripes,
dots, spatters, whatever you fancy.

· 1901 ·

Rent a cottage on an island, in the woods,
by a lake, or in a quaint little town.

· 1902 ·

Go on a hayride with a gang of friends.

· 1903 ·

Buy freshly made apple cider in the fall.
Drink it ice-cold.

· 1904 ·

Ask for samples at the cheese store.

· 1905 ·

Use ready-made piecrusts.

· 1906 ·

Build a kitchen pantry with lots of
shelves and cupboards.

· 1907 ·

Wear loose pants with elastic at the waist.

· 1908 ·

Wear pants that fit you like a glove.

· 1909 ·
Wear control-top pantyhose
for a sleek look.

🌸 *Give yourself a break:*
Put *your* needs first.

· 1911 ·
Strut your stuff.

· 1912 ·
Keep out of the midday sun.

· 1913 ·
Go for a swim on a sweltering night.

· 1914 ·
Don't take bad advice.

· 1915 ·
When sweet corn is in season, get yourself
as much as you can put away at one sitting.

· 1916 ·
When the nectarines are
perfectly ripe, eat them all.

· 1917 ·
Take a nap in a sweet-smelling
hayloft with the sun coming through
the little window.

· 1918 ·
Do more.

· 1919 ·
Do less.

· 1920 ·
Let your lover shampoo your
hair in the shower.

· 1921 ·
Go to a performance
under the stars.

· 1922 ·

Sit out on the fire escape
and enjoy the city night.

· 1923 ·

What's your secret passion? Act on it.

· 1924 ·

Play poker for fun instead of money.

 Do yourself a favor:
Let go of pointless grudges.

· 1926 ·

Set the scene for love: warmth, soft lights,
music, a bottle of wine.

· 1927 ·

Dip dried or glacé fruit (pears, nectarines,
peaches, pineapple) in melted chocolate;
put aside on waxed paper while
the chocolate sets. Enjoy.

· 1928 ·
Fly first class.

· 1929 ·
Try pedal boating.

· 1930 ·
Take a kayak out on a salt marsh
early in the morning. Paddle quietly
and look for waterbirds.

· 1931 ·
Go to the summer or winter Olympics.

✳ *Climb every mountain.*

✳ *Don't climb any mountain.*

· 1934 ·
Convert your anger to
constructive action.

· 1935 ·

Learn to say you're sorry, and mean it. You'll
feel like a very good person when you do.

· 1936 ·

Browse the humor section of your local
bookstore and buy yourself a funny book.

· 1937 ·

Have your walls wallpapered
instead of painted.

· 1938 ·

Have your car washed and polished.

· 1939 ·

Establish cordial relations
with your neighbors.

❋ *Give yourself a break:*
Send your kids to summer camp.

· 1941 ·
Treat yourself to a premium cable TV
channel for a few months.

· 1942 ·
Decide on a simpler Thanksgiving menu
this year, and stick to your guns.

· 1943 ·
Cook a *fresh* turkey instead of
a frozen one—delicious!

· 1944 ·
Use a disposable turkey-roasting pan,
and throw it out after the big meal.
No cleanup = pampering.

· 1945 ·
Have Thanksgiving dinner
at a restaurant.

· 1946 ·

On the day after Thanksgiving, start
your Christmas shopping.

· 1947 ·

On the day after Thanksgiving, stay
home in your pajamas instead of starting
your Christmas shopping.

٭ *Plan ahead for Christmas,
and feel completely organized
and totally on top of things.*

٭ *Don't plan ahead for
Christmas, and delight yourself
by improvising as you go along.*

· 1950 ·

Do your Christmas
shopping by catalog.

· 1951 ·

Learn about other winter celebrations:
Hanukkah, Kwanzaa, the winter solstice.

· 1952 ·

When you order holiday gifts for friends
and family, let the mail-order company
do the wrapping and mailing.

· 1953 ·

Throw out those battered,
blackened old cookie sheets and
buy new ones in time for baking
Christmas cookies.

· 1954 ·

Decorate with spirit
for the holidays.

· 1955 ·
Buy or make a fragrant herb
wreath to hang indoors. Bay leaves
are a good choice.

· 1956 ·
Stock up on old-fashioned
penny candy: jelly beans, gumdrops,
lemon drops, peppermint sticks,
malted milk balls, root beer barrels.

· 1957 ·
Buy your holiday cards
early and start addressing them
right away, so you don't have to
do them at the last minute.

· 1958 ·
Write a letter to Santa and leave
it in a conspicuous spot.

 * *Make a gingerbread house.*

 * *Don't make a gingerbread house.*

· 1961 ·

Hang a fresh pine wreath *inside* your house (in the kitchen, living room, den, TV room), so you can enjoy that special Christmas scent.

· 1962 ·

Put a dozen pots of poinsettia on your front porch.

· 1963 ·

Get rid of that fake Christmas tree and have a real one this year.

· 1964 ·

Instead of lugging it home yourself, have your tree delivered.

· 1965 ·

Make or buy some new and beautiful
ornaments for your tree.

· 1966 ·

Hire a car and driver
(possibly a teenaged one) to take
you from store to store until
your holiday shopping is *done*.

· 1967 ·

Have your holiday presents
wrapped at the store.

* *Go to the office Christmas
party.*

* *Don't go to the office
Christmas party.*

· 1970 ·

Get out of town:
Take a trip this holiday season
instead of coping with family,
friends, parties, crowds, anxiety.

· 1971 ·

Try an old-world Christmas treat:
panforte from Italy, Christmas pudding
from England, stollen from Germany,
sugarplums from Portugal.

· 1972 ·

Don't do the holiday shopping all by
yourself. Share the pleasure.

· 1973 ·

Buy yourself a decorated
cookie to nibble.

❀ *Do yourself a favor:*
Try not to spend more on
gifts than you can afford.

· 1975 ·
In addition to your big
Christmas tree, have a
small tree in the room where
you spend the most time—kitchen,
bedroom, den. Decorate it with
miniature ornaments.

· 1976 ·
If you're traveling to visit your family in
another part of the country, mail or ship
gifts ahead so you don't have to haul them
through airports and train stations.

· 1977 ·
Use convenience foods during the
holidays: take-out meals, ready-made
salads, desserts from the bakery.

· 1978 ·

Don't feel compelled to do all those
millions of things the magazines tell
you to do for the holidays.

· 1979 ·

Do one-stop shopping: Buy a book
for each person on your gift list.

· 1980 ·

Here's an easy-to-make centerpiece:
Put a fragrant balsam wreath flat on your
dining table; fill the center with chubby
red and white candles.

* *Bake Christmas cookies.*

* *Don't bake Christmas cookies.*

· 1983 ·
Roast chestnuts.

· 1984 ·
Ditch the fruitcake.

· 1985 ·
Send yourself a fabulous food
basket from a catalog.

· 1986 ·
Make a special drink for the holidays:
eggnog, mulled wine, champagne
punch, wassail, spiced cider.

· 1987 ·
Hang a mistletoe kissing ball,
so you'll be kissed.

· 1988 ·
Wear holiday finery at
every opportunity.

· 1989 ·

Turn off all the lights except the
Christmas tree lights. Sit on the
sofa and enjoy the magic.

· 1990 ·

Sing in a performance of
Handel's *Messiah*.

· 1991 ·

Give yourself a holiday present.

· 1992 ·

Drive through your town and
enjoy the decorations on your neighbors'
houses and lawns.

· 1993 ·

Attend the midnight service
on Christmas Eve.

· 1994 ·

See *The Nutcracker.*

· 1995 ·

Organize a caroling party, indoors or out.
Sing loud! Be joyous!

· 1996 ·

Stay home with your sweetie on
New Year's Eve.

❋ *Make a really good
New Year's resolution.*

❋ *Don't make a single
New Year's resolution.*

· 1999 ·

Spend New Year's Day with
friends. Invite the gang to
an afternoon open house.

· 2000 ·

Sprinkle your hair with glitter.

· 2001 ·

Put a welcome mat outside your door.